CRE▲TIVE
HOMEOWNER®

plumbing

step-by-step

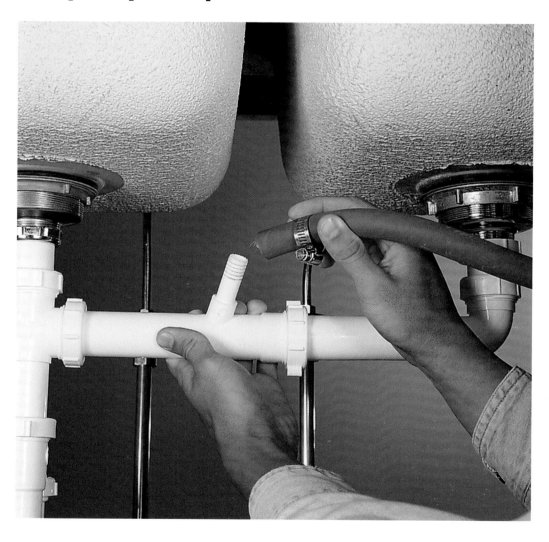

CREATIVE HOMEOWNER®, Upper Saddle River, New Jersey

COPYRIGHT © 2007, 2009

CRE▲TIVE
HOMEOWNER®

A Division of Federal Marketing Corp.
Upper Saddle River, NJ

SMARTGUIDE® and Creative Homeowner® are resgistered trademarks of Federal Marketing Corp.

SMART GUIDE: PLUMBING

MANAGING EDITOR	Fran Donegan
JUNIOR EDITOR	Angela Hanson
PROOFREADER	Sara Markowitz
TECHNICAL EDITOR	Merle Henkenius
GRAPHIC DESIGNER	Kathryn Wityk
PHOTO COORDINATOR	Mary Dolan
DIGITAL IMAGING SPECIALIST	Frank Dyer
INDEXER	Schroeder Indexing Services
SMART GUIDE® SERIES COVER DESIGN	Clarke Barre
FRONT COVER PHOTOGRAPHY	Merle Henkenius

CREATIVE HOMEOWNER

VICE PRESIDENT AND PUBLISHER	Timothy O. Bakke
MANAGING EDITOR	Fran J. Donegan
ART DIRECTOR	David Geer
PRODUCTION COORDINATOR	Sara M. Markowitz

Current Printing (last digit)
10 9 8 7 6 5 4 3 2 1

Manufactured in the United States of America

Smart Guide: Plumbing, Second Edition
Library of Congress Control Number: 2009921972
ISBN-10: 1-58011-464-4
ISBN-13: 978-1-58011-464-6

CREATIVE HOMEOWNER®
A Division of Federal Marketing Corp.
24 Park Way
Upper Saddle River, NJ 07458
www.creativehomeowner.com

Metric Conversion

Length

1 inch	25.4 mm
1 foot	0.3048 m
1 yard	0.9144 m
1 mile	1.61 km

Area

1 square inch	645 mm²
1 square foot	0.0929 m²
1 square yard	0.8361 m²
1 acre	4046.86 m²
1 square mile	2.59 km²

Volume

1 cubic inch	16.3870 cm³
1 cubic foot	0.03 m³
1 cubic yard	0.77 m³

Common Lumber Equivalents
Sizes: Metric cross sections are so close to their U.S. sizes, as noted below, that for most purposes they may be considered equivalents.

Dimensional lumber	1 x 2	19 x 38 mm
	1 x 4	19 x 89 mm
	2 x 2	38 x 38 mm
	2 x 4	38 x 89 mm
	2 x 6	38 x 140 mm
	2 x 8	38 x 184 mm
	2 x 10	38 x 235 mm
	2 x 12	38 x 286 mm
Sheet sizes	4 x 8 ft.	1200 x 2400 mm
	4 x 10 ft.	1200 x 3000 mm
Sheet thicknesses	¼ in.	6 mm
	⅜ in.	9 mm
	½ in.	12 mm
	¾ in.	19 mm
Stud/joist spacing	16 in. o.c.	400 mm o.c.
	24 in. o.c.	600 mm o.c.

Capacity

1 fluid ounce	29.57 mL
1 pint	473.18 mL
1 quart	1.14 L
1 gallon	3.79 L

Weight

1 ounce	28.35g
1 pound	0.45kg

Temperature
Celsius = Fahrenheit − 32 x ⁵⁄₉
Fahrenheit = Celsius x 1.8 + 32

Nail Size & Length

Penny Size	Nail Length
2d	1"
3d	1¼ in.
4d	1½ in.
5d	1¾ in.
6d	2 in.
7d	2¼ in.
8d	2½ in.
9d	2¾ in.
10d	3"
12d	3¼ in.
16d	3½ in.

contents

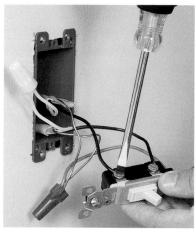

safety first

Though all the procedures in this book have been reviewed for safety, it is not possible to over-state the importance of using the safest construction methods possible. What follows are reminders; some do's and don'ts of basic how-to and plumbing work. They are not substitutes for your own common sense.

- Always use caution, care, and good judgment when following the procedures described in this book.

- Always obey *local* plumbing codes and laws, available from the building inspector. This book is based on the National Standard Plumbing Code, which despite its name, is one of several regional plumbing codes in force in the United States. As of the time of publication, there is no truly national plumbing code.

- Always use a flame shield to protect combustible materials when using a torch for soldering. And keep a fire extinguisher nearby whenever using a torch, just in case.

- Always be sure that the electrical setup is safe, that no circuit is overloaded, and that all power tools and outlets are properly grounded. Do not use power tools in wet locations. Use a battery powered flashlight when working near or with water.

- Always read labels on solvents and other products; provide ventilation; and observe all other warnings.

- Always read the manufacturer's instructions, especially the warnings, for using a tool or installing an appliance.

- Always remove the key from any drill chuck (portable or press) before starting the drill.

- Always use a drill with an auxiliary handle to control the torque when using large-size bits.

- Always pay deliberate attention to how a tool works so that you can avoid being injured.

- Always wear the appropriate rubber gloves or work gloves when handling chemicals, soldering, or doing heavy construction.

- Always wear a disposable face mask when you create dust by sawing or sanding. Use a special filtering respirator when working with toxic substances and solvents.

- Never try to light a gas appliance, like a water heater, if you smell gas. Do not touch any electrical switch or use any telephone in the same building. Go to a neighbor's house, and call the gas supplier. If you cannot reach your gas supplier, call the fire department.

- Always wear eye protection, especially when soldering, using a plunger or auger, using power tools, or striking metal on metal or concrete; a chip can fly off, for example, when chiseling concrete.

- Never work while wearing loose clothing, open cuffs, or jewelry; tie back long hair.

- Always be aware that there is seldom enough time for your body's reflexes to save you from injury from a power tool in a dangerous situation; everything happens too fast. Be alert!

- Always keep your hands away from the business ends of blades, cutters, and bits.

- Always hold a circular saw firmly, usually with both hands.

- Always check your local building codes when planning new construction. The codes are intended to protect public safety and should be observed to the letter.

- Never work with power tools when you are tired or when under the influence of alcohol or drugs.

- Never cut tiny pieces of pipe or wood using a power saw. When you need a small piece, saw it from a securely clamped longer piece.

- Never change a saw blade or a drill bit unless the power cord is unplugged. Do not depend on the switch being off. You might accidentally hit it.

- Always know the limitations of your tools. Do not try to force them to do what they were not designed to do.

- Never work in insufficient lighting.

- Never work with dull tools. Have them sharpened, or learn how to sharpen them yourself.

- Never use a power tool on a workpiece—large or small—that is not firmly supported.

- Never carry sharp or pointed tools, such as utility knives, awls, or chisels, in your pocket. If you want to carry any of these tools, use a special-purpose tool belt that has leather pockets and holders.

Plumbing Made Simple

These are good times for do-it-yourself plumbers. Plumbing materials are lighter and easier than ever to install, and the range of quality products sold to home-owners is unprecedented. Fifteen years ago, many of these products were sold only through wholesalers to plumbers.

And the materials are affordable. Many faucets and fixtures cost less at home centers than they do at wholesale houses. This may be bad news for plumbers, but it's good news for you. With these advantages, all you need is help with the installations. That is the purpose of this book.

Smart Guide: Plumbing is loaded with detailed projects, but it also provides context. The first chapter provides the background needed to accomplish almost any plumbing task, from the materials and tools needed to the importance of vents and traps in a properly functioning plumbing system. There is also information here for laying out plumbing systems.

From there the book examines some component of a typical residential system, providing the information you need to make repairs and improve an existing system. There are chapters on working with drain-pipes made of different materials and cutting and soldering copper water pipes, as well as working with plastic water and drainpipes. *Smart Guide: Plumbing* also examines Pex, a cross-linked polyethylene piping system as well.

You can use the information in those chapters to make practical repairs and upgrades to your home. Step-by-step photo sequences will lead you through removing and installing sinks, faucets, and shower-heads. Learn to fix leaks in all of the types of faucets on the market today. Install a new toilet or fix the one you have now. There are even sections on installing waste-disposal units and dishwashers.

About Plumbing Codes. Many plumbing projects require permits, so *Smart Guide: Plumbing* is based on industry standards and code compliance, project by project. All projects in the book are based on the National Standard Plumbing Code, which despite its name is one of several regional plumbing codes, along with countless local codes, in force in the United States. As a practical matter, the only codes that really matter are those adopted by your local municipality. You'll learn enough about the fundamentals to work intelligently with your codes office. So be sure to check in with the local code authority before starting a plumbing project.

Learn to replace a tub and shower faucet, install a bathtub, fix leaky faucets, install a new toilet, and much more.

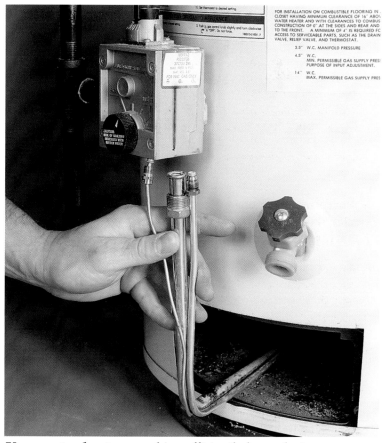

Keep water heaters working efficiently by replacing or repairing damaged parts and components.

plumbing basics

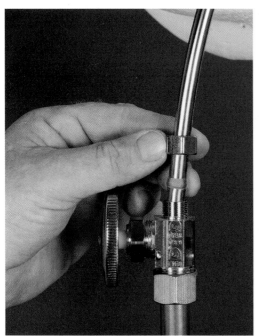

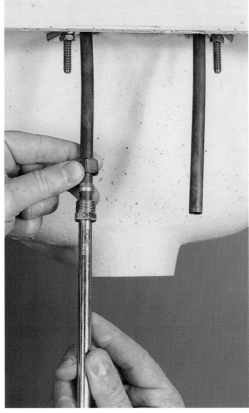

Plumbing Systems

A home's plumbing system, with its tangle of pipes appearing here and disappearing there, can be daunting. If you think your plumbing system looks like a can of worms and it's completely unapproachable, take heart. It's really not as complicated as it appears. In fact, the entire system is comprehensible if you take a few minutes to organize the confusion into manageable segments, according to function.

Even if you go only so far as to separate the incoming water pipes from the outgoing drainage pipes, most of the battle is won. Separating these two systems is easy because the pipe sizes are different. Drainpipes are larger than water pipes, ranging between 1¼ and 4 inches in diameter. Water pipes are typically ½ and ¾ inch in diameter. These are inside diameters, so exterior measurements will be a little larger.

SMART TIP

Digging in public property. Although you're charged with maintaining the sidewalk in front of your house and the space, if any, between the sidewalk and street, this area is really public property. It's sometimes known as the public parking, and any qualified person needing to work on buried pipes can dig in this ground, even if it seems to be part of your lawn. You have a right to dig across the street to make installations and repairs, and your neighbor from across the street has the right to dig on your side. There is no need to tear up an area of more than about 4 by 8 feet. Whoever does the digging, whether by hand or machine, should also try to restore the grass.

To get a sense of how plumbing systems work, it helps to follow the route that fresh water takes as it enters your home, passes through your fixtures and appliances, and drains to your septic system or public sewer.

Water Supply System

Each home has a water service pipe that travels underground from its supply source—either a private well and pump or public water main. Service lines are buried between 1 and 6 feet deep, depending on climate. The colder the climate, the deeper the lines are buried. City water services typically have three or four shutoff valves, offering several points at which to interrupt service. Only the last two valves are readily accessible to homeowners, however.

Common Plumbing Tools

(A) soldering torch
(B) blow bag
(C) pipe-cleaning tool
(D) hand auger
(E) standard plunger
(F) combination plunger
(G) handle puller
(H) closet auger

Municipal Supply Lines

The first shutoff in the water line is actually part of the water-main tap mechanism, in which a motorized tapping machine has bored a self-tapping valve directly into an iron or plastic water main. The tap/valve, once in place, is called a *corporation stop*, or more commonly, a *corpcock*. You can reach it only by excavating the soil above it.

The second shutoff is also underground, usually in the public area between the street and sidewalk. The term for this in-line valve is a *curb stop*. It's only accessible with a long street key—which plumbers carry—and has a pipelike sleeve that reaches to grade level. This vertical extension is called a *stopbox*. If you've been mowing around a protruding stopbox for years, you should know that it is adjustable, up or down. Call a plumber to adjust it.

A final pair of valves connects directly to the water meter, although in some houses there is only one valve. The valve on the street side of the meter is called a *meter valve* and the one on the house side, a *house valve*. These are the valves you'll use to shut down the system for emergencies and repairs, so it pays to know where your meter is located and how to reach both valves.

Where are the Water and Sewer Mains Hidden?

Water and sewer mains are usually located near the street curb, with the sewer on one side of the street and the water on the other. Plumbers usually have to bore under the street with a mechanical boring machine to reach a main. Both mains need to be unearthed to make the service connections. Water mains are usually 3 to 6 feet deep, while sewers are between 3 and 15 feet deep, with most in the 8- to 10-foot range.

In older neighborhoods, city mains may be located under the street. To gain access for installations or repairs, you must cut out a section of street. Street repair costs generally accrue to the homeowner. In the oldest neighborhoods, sewers are often located in alleyways. Your town's public works department should be able to tell you exactly where your sewer and water mains lie.

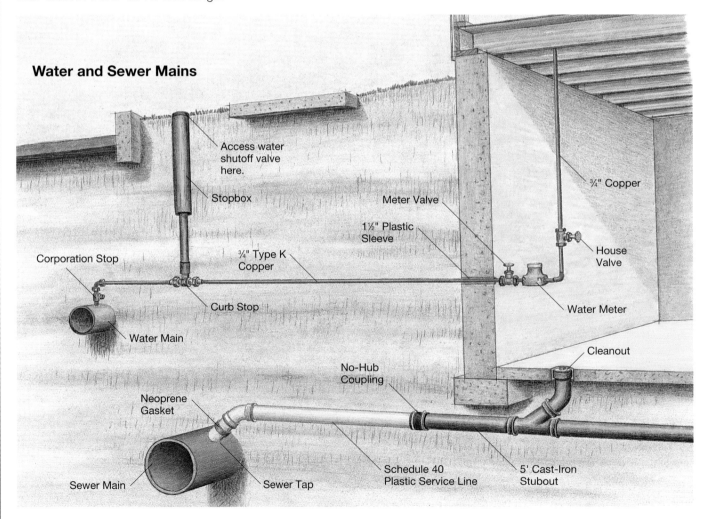

Water and Sewer Mains

- Access water shutoff valve here.
- Stopbox
- Meter Valve
- 1½" Plastic Sleeve
- ¾" Copper
- Corporation Stop
- ¾" Type K Copper
- House Valve
- Curb Stop
- Water Meter
- Water Main
- Cleanout
- No-Hub Coupling
- Neoprene Gasket
- Sewer Main
- Sewer Tap
- Schedule 40 Plastic Service Line
- 5' Cast-Iron Stubout

The Midcentury Benchmark

The 1950s were watershed years in home building, with methods and materials changing dramatically. A house built in the 1950s not only looks different from its 1940s predecessor, it is in fact built differently. In the 1950s, balloon framing was out; platform framing was in. Plaster was out; drywall was in. Knob-and-tube wiring was out; sheathed cable was in. Galvanized-steel piping was out; copper piping was in. And so on.

The end of World War II had a great deal to do with these changes. Thousands of returning young soldiers sought affordable housing through the GI Bill as they settled down to start families. Builders began to use mass-production building methods to meet the demand for housing, and once-rationed materials of every description were readily available. Not surprisingly, some of the 1950s tract homes, furrowed in neat rows, bore a noticeable resemblance to military-base housing. In any case, this midcentury benchmark is useful when assessing the best approach for repairs and upgrades. Different methods and materials require different approaches.

Water Meters

The water meter marks the end of the service line and the beginning of the in-house plumbing system. In some cases, the city owns the meters, while in others, users buy and maintain them at their own expense. Meters are usually inside the house, in a utility room, basement, or crawlspace, but some are outside, buried in *meter pits*. Meter pits are usually near the street, on either side of the sidewalk. If the meter is in a pit, the system rarely has a curb stop. In this case, the system has an additional valve just inside or outside the house, depending on the climate.

Types of Service Line

Service Lines in Older Homes. In homes built before World War II, the original service line is usually galvanized steel with a ¾-inch inside diameter. Pipes predating 1930 may terminate in a lead pipe loop. To identify a lead loop, look for a blackish gray pipe that curves between the meter valve and the galvanized-steel service line. You should see a bulge at each end where the loop joins the pipe and meter valve. These hand-formed splices are called *wiped-lead joints* and are now a lost art. Plumbers made them using candle wax and molten lead, sweeping the lead repeatedly around the joint with the aid of a heat-resistant glove.

Plumbers also used lead underground at the water main because it was soft enough to accommodate seasonal ground movement. If you see a lead loop at the meter-end of your service line, expect one at the other end as well. While clearly obsolete, millions of lead loops are still in place, even though lead is now known to be extremely toxic. In most cases, mineral deposits sealed the water from the lead long ago.

Service Lines in Newer Homes. Homes built after 1950 have soft-copper service pipes. Again, the predominate size was ¾ inch, though larger diameters—up to 1¼ inch—were sometimes used to compensate for low pressure. Today 1-inch services are common, especially when plans include underground sprinkler systems. If your system draws water from a recently installed private well, expect to see plastic pipes in place, 1 to 1¼ inches in diameter. Most plumbers place a shutoff valve on the well side of the pressure tank. (Never shut off this valve without also shutting off power to the pump.)

Lead Pipe Loop

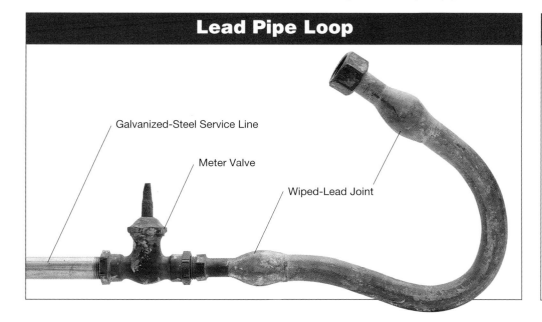

Galvanized-Steel Service Line

Meter Valve

Wiped-Lead Joint

SMART TIP

Free up floor space in a small bathroom or powder room where a conventional toilet will get in the way by installing a corner toilet. These units have a wedge-shaped tank that fits neatly into an inside corner. You will still need to run standard-size supply lines and drain pipe. The rough-in for the toilet is 12½ inches from the rough framing of the walls.

Interior Water Supply Systems

A home's in-house water system starts with the water meter or, in the case of a private well, a pressure tank. If your home has an outdoor meter pit, consider the first full-size shutoff valve in the house as the starting point. From here, a single supply line—the cold-water trunk line—travels to a central location where a T-fitting splits it into two lines. One of these enters the top of a water heater while the other continues to feed cold water to the house. A third line exits the heater and becomes the system's hot-water trunk line. The hot-and-cold-water trunk lines usually run side by side along the center beam of the house, branching to serve isolated fixtures or fixture groups along the way.

In most cases, the trunk lines are ¾ inch in diameter and run under the floor joists, near the beam. The branch lines are usually tucked up between the joists so that most of the basement ceiling can be finished. While trunk lines are typically ¾ inch in diameter, branch lines are usually reduced to ½ inch in diameter at some point. Most codes allow only two fixtures on a ½-inch line, so plumbers will run ¾-inch branch lines until they reach the third-to-last fixture on the run. They also reduce to ½ inch in diameter on the dedicated fixture risers that extend directly from the trunk lines.

No Basement?

Where are the water pipes if you live in a house without a basement? It depends on the type of home. If your ground floor spans a crawl space, the piping is likely to resemble that of a basement installation, except that the water heater may be located on the main floor in a utility closet.

If yours is a slab-on-grade home with a concrete floor, expect to find soft-copper water piping buried under the concrete slab. The water service in this case will usually enter a utility room through the floor. In most cases, the fixture supply piping will also be run under the slab, surfacing in the utility room near the meter on one end, and near each fixture or group of fixtures on the other. In the extreme southern reaches of the country, where hard freezes are unlikely, copper or plastic water lines may be run in the attic, with branch lines dropping into plumbing walls.

Water Supply Lines

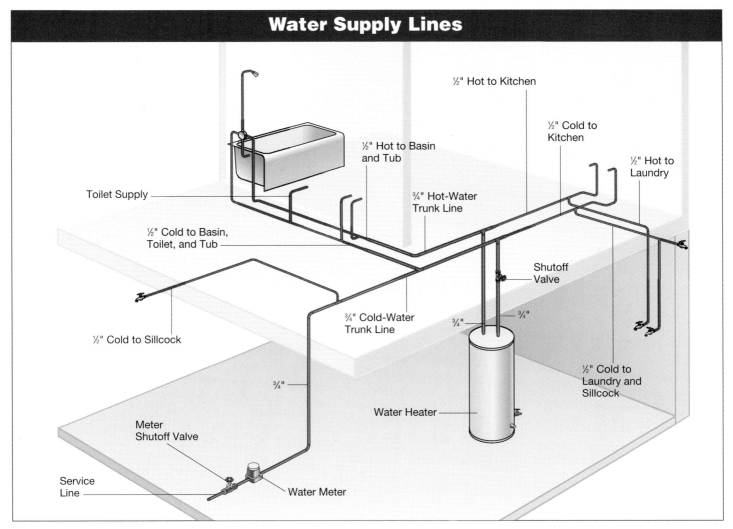

½" Hot to Kitchen

½" Cold to Kitchen

½" Hot to Laundry

½" Hot to Basin and Tub

¾" Hot-Water Trunk Line

Toilet Supply

½" Cold to Basin, Toilet, and Tub

Shutoff Valve

¾" Cold-Water Trunk Line

¾"

¾"

½" Cold to Sillcock

¾"

½" Cold to Laundry and Sillcock

Water Heater

Meter Shutoff Valve

Service Line

Water Meter

Drainage & Vent Systems

A plumbing drainage system has three basic segments, each with its own function: drainpipes, vent pipes, and fixture traps.

■ *Drainpipes* direct wastewater away from the fixtures and house to the sewer, septic tank, or cesspool.

■ *Vent pipes* allow air to enter the drainage system to equalize air pressure, allowing the wastewater to flow freely and prevent suction.

■ *Fixture traps* hold a small amount of water at fixtures to prevent the passage of sewer gas and vermin from the drainpipes into a living area.

Unlike potable-water systems, which flow under pressure, waste systems operate by gravity. Consequently, designers of these fittings emphasize gradual flow patterns and broad sweeps instead of abrupt turns. The abrupt geometry of water fittings is too severe for drain fittings. It's a difference you can see.

Sizes and Materials

As noted earlier, drainpipes are larger than water pipes, ranging in diameter from 1¼ to 4 inches. Any pipe 1½ inches in diameter or larger is likely to be a drainpipe or vent pipe; most 1¼-inch pipes are drainpipes only. Galvanized steel, copper, cast iron, and plastic are all common drainage and vent-pipe materials. The 1950s and 1960s also saw the installation of a good many copper and brass systems. After the mid-1970s, drain/vent systems usually tended to be plastic.

The Drainpipe System

The in-house waste drainage system starts with a main pipe several feet outside an exterior wall, which passes under the house footing and into the basement or crawlspace. This below-floor drainpipe, usually 4 inches in diameter, is called the *main soil pipe*. The main soil pipe continues horizontally under the basement floor or slab (or along a wall), sometimes branching off—and reducing—to serve a laundry standpipe or maybe a floor drain or two. Where the main soil pipe runs under the basement floor, it terminates in a 90-degree sweep bend through the floor and becomes the base for the primary vertical stack, or the main stack.

Drain and Vent Lines

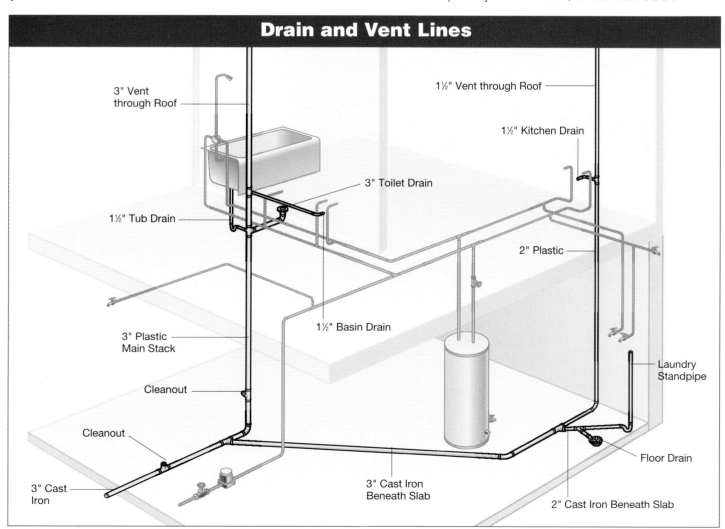

3" Vent through Roof

1½" Vent through Roof

1½" Kitchen Drain

3" Toilet Drain

1½" Tub Drain

2" Plastic

1½" Basin Drain

3" Plastic Main Stack

Cleanout

Laundry Standpipe

Cleanout

Floor Drain

3" Cast Iron

3" Cast Iron Beneath Slab

2" Cast Iron Beneath Slab

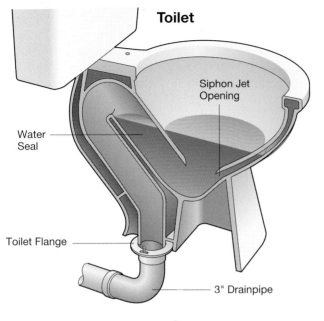

Toilet

Siphon Jet Opening

Water Seal

Toilet Flange

3" Drainpipe

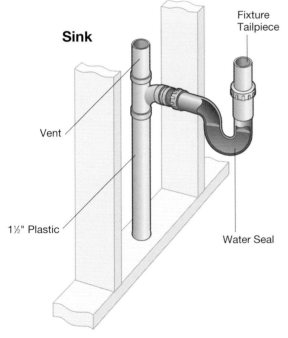

Sink

Fixture Tailpiece

Vent

1½" Plastic

Water Seal

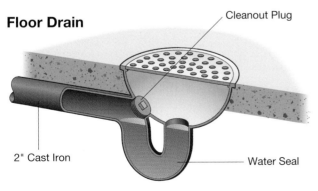

Floor Drain

Cleanout Plug

2" Cast Iron

Water Seal

Drain Traps. Each fixture in the system is joined to its branch line via a water trap. These are critical components because they hold back the considerable volume of sewer gas present in every sewer system. While every fixture and drain must have a trap, not all traps are the same. Toilets, for example, have built-in, or *integral*, traps. The water you see standing in a toilet bowl is trapped there by an outlet passage that sweeps up before it sweeps down to its drainpipe connection. Floor drains also have integral traps, as do bidets and some urinals.

Sinks have sharply curved external chrome or plastic tube traps (P-traps), which can be disassembled for service work. Tub, shower, and laundry traps, in contrast, are usually fixed one-piece units, which are difficult to service.

Vent Pipes. Vents are important to a drainage system because they allow traps and drains to function properly. When water flows from a fixture through a pipe, it displaces an amount of air equal to its own volume, creating negative pressure behind the flow. This localized suction can be quite strong, especially at bends in the pipe. A toilet flushing near a sink, for example, can easily pull water from the sink's P-trap, allowing poisonous sewer gas into the living quarters. In fact, without adequate venting, a toilet won't flush properly.

Every home needs a stack vent through the roof, of course, but that's not always enough. All sorts of common situations can choke a vent, so it's necessary to have auxiliary vents, called *re-vents*. The shape, size, and location of these vents are critically important.

Fixtures. The point of all this piping begins and ends with the fixtures: sinks, toilets, tubs, and shower stalls. Fixtures are not as permanent as they appear. They are designed to be taken up and put back with relative ease and at moderate expense. Even bathtubs, which can look as though they've grown right out of the structural timbers of a home, are not that difficult to replace. If an old or defective fixture has you mumbling to yourself with every use, don't be intimidated: tear it out and put in a new one.

Appliances. The list of plumbing-related appliances has grown over the years to include water heaters, dishwashers, water softeners, water purifiers, clothes washers (which are not really plumbed in), waste-disposal units, hot-water dispensers, whirlpool tubs—and even refrigerators, with their ice makers. However, only the water heater is an essential and code-required part of every home's plumbing system.

Types of Pipe

Characteristics	Cutting Tools	Joining Method
PVC Pipe. Polyvinyl chloride plastic pipe is the preferred drain and vent piping for houses. It can't corrode, and it's easy to assemble.	Wheel cutter, hacksaw, scissor cutter	PVC solvent cement
ABS Pipe. Acrylonitrile butadiene styrene is a black plastic used in the same applications as PVC. It is not as rigid as PVC.	Wheel cutter, hacksaw	ABS or PVC solvent cement
Cast-Iron Pipe. Once used in drain and vent systems, this durable but brittle metal pipe has been largely replaced by PVC and ABS plastic.	Snap cutter, chisel	Banded neoprene couplings or rubber gaskets
Rigid Copper Pipe. The dominant water piping material today, copper pipe is usually joined with soldered (sweat) fittings.	Wheel cutter, hacksaw	Sweat or compression fittings
Soft Copper Pipe. Used primarily for natural gas and propane but also for water, this pipe is allowed under concrete.	Wheel cutter, hacksaw	Compression, solder, or flare fittings
Chromed Copper Tubing. This flexible piping is used as fixture water-supply tubes between fixtures and permanent piping.	Wheel cutter, hacksaw	Compression fittings
Flexible Braided-Steel Supply Line. This flexible piping, often used as fixture supply tubing, is easier to use than chromed copper tubing.	Fixed length	Factory-installed fittings
Chromed Ribbed Copper Pipe. Available only as fixture supply tubing, the ribbed section of this pipe makes it easy to bend.	Can't cut	Compression fittings
CPVC Pipe. Chlorinated polyvinyl chloride plastic water piping was created to replace rigid copper. Does not meet all local codes.	Wheel cutter, hacksaw, or scissor cutter	PVC cement or compression or crimp ring fittings
Pex Pipe. Cross-linked polyethylene plastic pipe is a flexible piping material gaining acceptance for in-house water systems. It requires few fittings.	Scissor tool, hacksaw	Several brands of proprietary fittings
Galvanized-Steel Pipe. Once used for in-house water systems, steel pipe is now used mostly in repair situations.	Wheel cutter and threading dies	Threaded fittings
Black Steel Pipe. Steel pipe was once used for in-house gas piping, though it's fast losing ground to soft copper and CSST.	Wheel cutter and threading dies	Threaded fittings
CSST. Corrugated stainless-steel tubing is a flexible, plastic-coated pipe made of stainless steel for in-house natural gas and propane.	Hacksaw or wheel cutter	Proprietary compression fittings

Fittings: (A) ¾ x ½ x ½-in. T-fitting, (B) drop-eared elbow, (C) brass union, (D) 90-deg. street elbow, (E) dielectric union, (F) copper sweat cap, (G) sweat × female adapter, (H) pipe strap, (I) repair coupling, (J) coupling, (K) reducing coupling, (L) ¾ x ½ x ¾-in. T-fitting, (M) ¾-in. T-fitting, (N) ½ x ½ x ¾-in. T-fitting, (O) ¾ x ¾ x ½-in. T-fitting, (P) 45-deg. street elbow, (Q) sweat × male adapter, (R) 90-deg. elbow, (S) 45-deg. elbow

Friction and Compression Fittings

Cone washers were common before compression fittings.

Modern installations use brass compression valves and fittings.

Compression valves are also available with pipe threads.

Types of Supply Tubes

The ball head of this water supply tube crushes against the faucet shank.

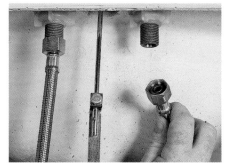

Flexible braided-steel water supply tubes come equipped with factory-installed fittings.

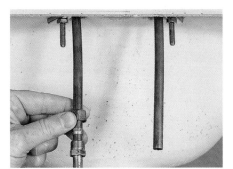

Compression coupling tubes are often used for faucets that have built-in supply tubes.

Making Plans

If you are planning to make improvements that require installation of plumbing fixtures or appliances where there are no water or drainage facilities, draw up a detailed plan to scale before proceeding. Once you have prepared the plan (along with a list of materials), have someone with experience doing similar projects check to see whether you have overlooked anything. The local plumbing-supply store may have trained consultants on staff who can provide this service. The two main tasks ahead of you will be, 1) to make sure your plans comply with code, and 2) to make accurate rough-in measurements.

Building Codes

A building code is a collection of legal statutes that specify which building materials may be used and how these materials are to be assembled in the construction of residential and commercial buildings. A code office has legal authority within its jurisdiction, be it state, county, or municipality. A typical building code covers everything from framing to concrete installations to ventilation and insulation. To comply with code, you must secure a building permit from the local building department and allow the building inspector or inspectors access to the work for inspection and approval at various stages of completion.

Lack of Uniformity. Unlike electrical codes, which are written at the national level (the National Electrical Code, or NEC) and enforced (and sometimes modified) at the state, county, and city level, plumbing codes are often written and enforced only at the city or county level. So while electricians normally carry both state and county licenses, plumbers are usually licensed only at the city/county level. Plumbers who work in more than one county or city must often have more than one license.

Many small towns and rural areas remain entirely without plumbing codes. More and more codes are going on the books in these areas, but the conversion is far from complete and may never be. The most far-reaching enforcement bodies are state and county health departments, which have little to do with home construction but claim jurisdiction over private wells and septic systems. You should check with the local building department to see what plumbing codes, if any, are enforced.

Properties financed with the aid of government guarantees, such as those of the U.S. Department of Housing and Urban Development's Federal Housing Administration (FHA) and the U.S. Department of Veterans Affairs (VA), must meet the guidelines established by these agencies in addition to meeting any applicable state, county, and municipal codes. These federal guidelines are not considered codes, however, and have more to do with home financing than home building.

Grandfather Clause to the Rescue

If you're like many homeowners, what keeps you from applying for permits and calling for inspections is the fear that once an inspector darkens your door, he or she will storm through the house condemning everything in sight. Is this possible? Perhaps, but it's not likely. Unless inspectors see something that is clearly a health hazard, there isn't much they can do.

If you have water running properly to the basic fixtures, reasonably few appliances plugged into working electrical outlets, no missing steps, and walls and a roof that appear as if they'll stay put, you are pretty much covered by the grandfather clause. The clause basically applies common sense by stating that new standards cannot be applied to old work unless that work now poses a genuine health risk to inhabitants or passersby. If older installations met the standards of their day, they will do until you decide to improve them. When you make those improvements, however, current standards will apply.

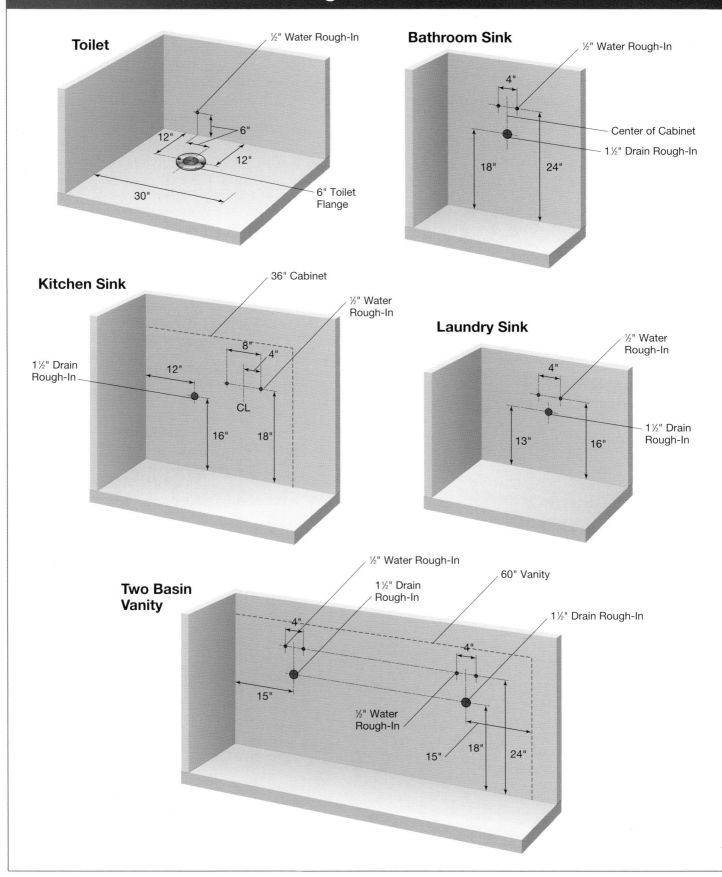

Toilet

½" Water Rough-In

12"

6"

12"

30"

6" Toilet Flange

Bathroom Sink

½" Water Rough-In

4"

Center of Cabinet

1½" Drain Rough-In

18"

24"

Kitchen Sink

36" Cabinet

½" Water Rough-In

1½" Drain Rough-In

12"

8"

4"

CL

16"

18"

Laundry Sink

½" Water Rough-In

4"

13"

16"

1½" Drain Rough-In

Two Basin Vanity

½" Water Rough-In

1½" Drain Rough-In

60" Vanity

1½" Drain Rough-In

4"

4"

15"

½" Water Rough-In

15"

18"

24"

Bathtub

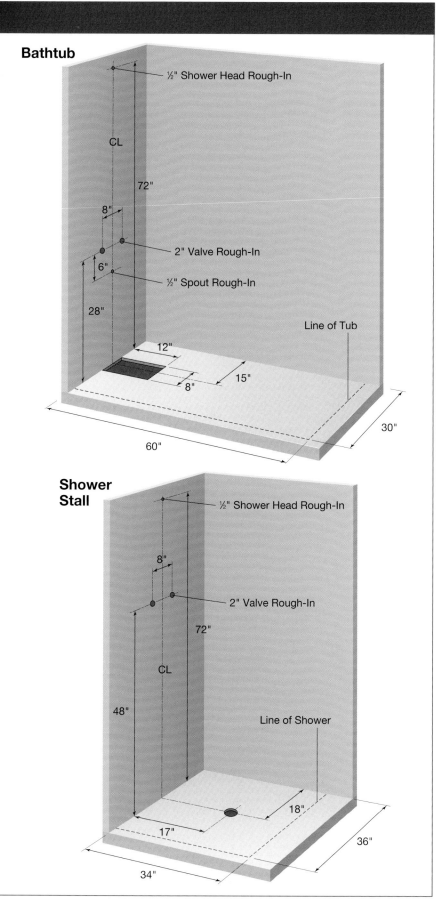

½" Shower Head Rough-In

CL

72"

8"

2" Valve Rough-In

6"

½" Spout Rough-In

28"

Line of Tub

12"

15"

8"

30"

60"

Shower Stall

½" Shower Head Rough-In

8"

2" Valve Rough-In

72"

CL

48"

Line of Shower

18"

17"

36"

34"

Permits and Inspections

If you're planning to install a permanent appliance like a water heater or to make a plumbing upgrade that will require piping changes or additions, visit the local building department and apply for a permit. You may be asked several questions about how you plan to accomplish this work, but don't be intimidated. Explain exactly what plumbing is in place and how you plan to expand or change it. If your plan is not likely to meet applicable codes, the code official will most likely be ready with suggestions to make it code-worthy.

Once you have worked out the details of your plan, you'll need to fill out a permit application. The form will probably have a list of fixtures and project descriptions. In most cases, you'll simply check the boxes next to each appropriate fixture or work category. If you plan to remodel a bathroom, for example, check the boxes next to Sink, Toilet, and Tub/Shower. The cost of the permit is usually determined by the number of boxes you check, but don't let this intimidate you. Permit fees are seldom expensive, especially for simple upgrades.

Inspections. You'll need to call for an inspection, usually a minimum of a day ahead of time, at the completion of each stage of work. Try to set up a time when you can meet the inspector on the job. At the very least, arrange for a friend or family member to open the door for him or her.

Just how many plumbing inspections will you need? It depends. If your remodeling involves in-wall piping and fixture installations, you'll need two inspections—a rough-in inspection and a finish inspection. But if you're simply replacing a water heater, where all of your work will be visible at a glance, then only a final inspection will be necessary. (New-home construction usually requires four plumbing inspections: one for the underground sewer and water service lines and taps, one after the installation of any under-slab or basement floor piping, another after the installation of above-floor rough-in piping, and a final inspection when the work is complete.)

Remember that an inspector must approve all in-wall and underground work before you cover it up. A building inspector has the authority to make you remove drywall, soil, or even concrete if he or she suspects substandard work. Covering your work prior to inspection automatically makes it suspicious.

chapter 2

drainpipes

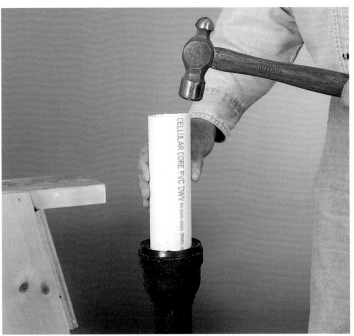

Drainage Systems

Drainpipes have the important job of carrying all the wastewater a household generates away from the house and into a sewer or septic system.

The sewer or septic system creates a poisonously gaseous environment, however, and all that stands between you and that environment is the water in your fixture traps. If you lose the water in one of these traps (by evaporation, suction, or some other means), noxious sewer gases will rise into your living quarters, possibly causing headaches and even respiratory illnesses in those exposed to the gases. This is why traps are so important in your drainage system.

A properly designed venting system is the only way to ensure that you maintain adequate water flow in drainpipes and water levels in fixture traps, so vents are also vitally important.

Drains

The drawing on the following page shows a typical plumbing system. Imagine that this is a one-story ranch-style home, with one bath on the main floor and another in the basement. The water piping is included to give a greater sense of perspective and detail. While not every house will be plumbed just like this one and codes may vary slightly, this is a good example of a code-worthy piping schematic.

Basic Drainage Considerations

Establishing an easy, gradual flow of wastewater is the prime consideration with drains. (Similarly, airflow is the critical, overriding objective of venting, which is essential to proper drainage.) Therefore, every drainpipe, whether buried under soil or threaded through walls, must be sloped just right. When installing drainpipes, shoot for a slope of 1/4 inch per foot. If structural barriers force a compromise, try to maintain at least 1/16 inch per foot.

Too Much Slope. As you've seen, a drain must slope downward if water is to flow by gravity, but you may not know that it's possible to have too much slope. When water moves through a horizontal pipe too quickly and that water is carrying solids, the water can outrun the solids. This is especially true of longer drain lines, such as the sewer service pipe between the house and sewer main. New low-flush toilets only compound the problem because they use less water. Even gray water—water that doesn't carry solids—leaves grease, soap, hair, and food particles behind when it moves through the system too quickly. Eventually these accumulations can cause the line to clog.

To prevent accumulation problems,

Plastic Drainage Piping

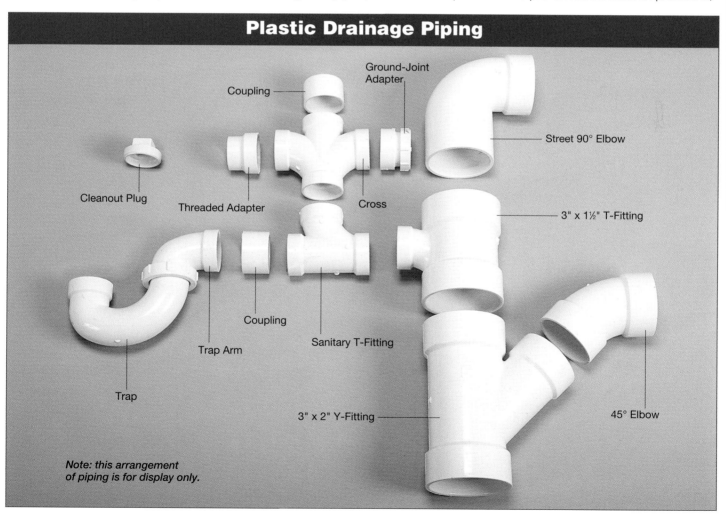

Coupling

Ground-Joint Adapter

Cleanout Plug

Threaded Adapter

Cross

Street 90° Elbow

3" x 1½" T-Fitting

Coupling

Trap Arm

Sanitary T-Fitting

Trap

3" x 2" Y-Fitting

45° Elbow

Note: this arrangement of piping is for display only.

Typical Drainage System

Working backward—that is, starting with where the wastewater exits the house—the drainage system begins with the 4-inch soil pipe, which enters the house under an exterior footing or slab. (In some cases the soil pipe may enter the house through the basement or crawl space wall, especially in a septic-system arrangement.) Just after the cleanout, a 4 x 2-inch Y-fitting splits off to drain the laundry in the basement and the kitchen on the main floor. Codes often require that this takeoff be downstream of the larger toilet-branch line.

The next in-line fitting is a 4-inch Y-fitting that serves the basement bath group—toilet, tub, and sink. The toilet line is re-vented because it is a lower floor installation; it does double duty as a wet vent for the shower and sink.

Before the soil pipe sweeps up to become the primary 3-inch vertical stack, an unvented 2-inch Y-fitting serves a trapped floor drain. On the stack, a 3-inch T-fitting with a 1½-inch side inlet serves the toilet and shower. The fitting allows both fixtures to enter the stack at the same level and, therefore, allows both to be stack-vented.

Approximately 16 inches above the floor, a second T-fitting drains the sink basin, which is also stack-vented. From the top of this T, the stack continues through the roof.

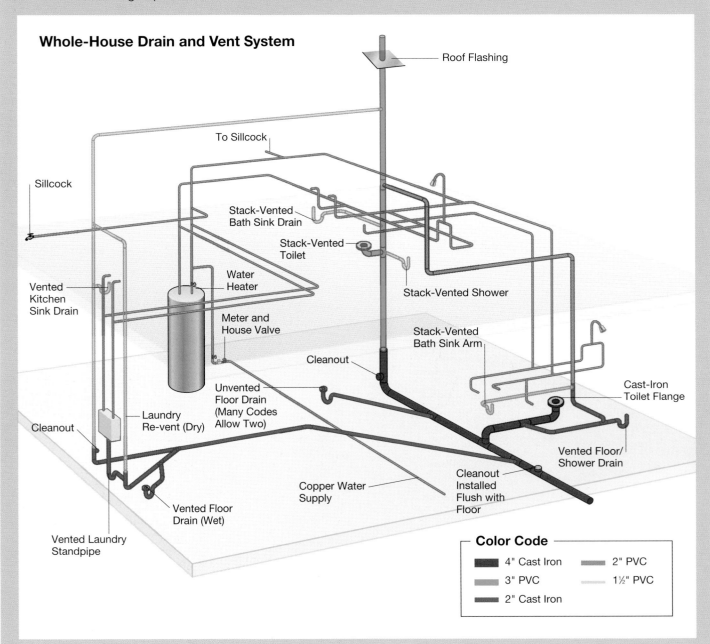

Whole-House Drain and Vent System

- Roof Flashing
- To Sillcock
- Sillcock
- Stack-Vented Bath Sink Drain
- Stack-Vented Toilet
- Stack-Vented Shower
- Water Heater
- Vented Kitchen Sink Drain
- Meter and House Valve
- Stack-Vented Bath Sink Arm
- Cleanout
- Unvented Floor Drain (Many Codes Allow Two)
- Cast-Iron Toilet Flange
- Cleanout
- Laundry Re-vent (Dry)
- Vented Floor/ Shower Drain
- Vented Floor Drain (Wet)
- Copper Water Supply
- Cleanout Installed Flush with Floor
- Vented Laundry Standpipe

Color Code

- ■ 4" Cast Iron
- ■ 3" PVC
- ■ 2" Cast Iron
- ■ 2" PVC
- ▬ 1½" PVC

limit the fall of any drain line to no more than ¼ inch per foot. If structural barriers force a slope greater than ¼ inch per foot or if the line will slope a distance greater than its own diameter along its length, use fittings to step up the line. Hold the line before and after the step at ⅛ to ¼ inch per foot. You must re-vent any line that slopes, from start to finish, more than its own diameter.

Fitting and pipe selection is also important. In a waste system, use only code-approved sanitary fittings. Do not use T-fittings in drainpipes except to drain and stack-vent the top fixture or the top bath group on a stack. A Y-connector, used in combination with a 45-degree elbow, offers a much more gradual flow, which is less likely to clog. This is true whether the stack is vertical or horizontal.

When you install a 90-degree elbow at the base of a vertical stack, use a long-sweep L configuration, or install two 45-degree elbows. Standard short-sweep elbows will do fine elsewhere in the system, but water falling vertically from a height of 8 to 24 feet needs a buffer as it changes direction. A more gradual turn will keep water from filling the elbow completely and prevent a momentary loss of vent.

When you install plastic drain and vent pipe—above or below the basement floor—make sure that it has a Schedule 40 rating. While codes once allowed thinner-walled pipe in underground sewer service lines, most codes today require Schedule 40 throughout, from sewer to roof.

Supporting Pipe. When you run pipe through stud walls or through floor and ceiling joists, always drill the pipe holes slightly larger than the outside diameter of the pipe. Plastic pipe expands when warm water passes through it, and if the pipe fits too tightly, you'll hear a steady ticking sound when warm water is used. This annoying sound is the pipe rubbing against the wood as the plastic expands and contracts.

When you hang plastic drainpipes and vent pipes under floor joists, support the pipe with hole strapping or the appropriate pipe hangers. Support plastic waste piping at least every 4 feet. (See photograph, below left.)

Cutting Structural Timbers. You'll rarely need to cut into load-bearing timbers to install drainpipes. You can usually hang a horizontal fixture line (extending from a vertical stack) under the joists near the center beam of the house and box the area in later. When a drain line needs to travel with the joists toward an outside wall, you can usually tuck it up between the joists.

You may need to run pipes through a few joists. This is usually not a problem, but with dimension lumber drill only the center one-third of each joist, and where possible, stay within a few feet of a support wall. Never notch the bottom of a joist, because the bottom carries a disproportionate share of the load. Engineered lumber has different drilling requirements, so check with the manufacturer.

The best approach is to use a right-angle drill equipped with a self-feed bit. Lacking these, drill four small holes to form a square (or circle), and cut between them using a reciprocating saw. Remember that each succeeding hole must be slightly higher (or lower) than the last to maintain an adequate slope. With 1½-inch pipe, you can often bend it enough to start it through the first two holes. After that, drive it through with a hammer, using a block of wood to protect the pipe. With larger pipes, you'll have to splice short lengths together using couplings, one coupling per joist space.

Wire hangers, which you just hammer into joists to support pipes, are quick and affordable. Several other types of hangers are available.

Use a right-angle drill and a large self-feed bit to bore pipe holes in studs. Make the holes at least ⅛ in. oversize.

Drill four holes if you don't have a large bit or hole saw.

Use a saber saw to cut out the lumber between the holes.

Fit short pieces of pipe between joists, and couple them together.

Installing In-Ground Piping

Every plumbing system has some portion of its drainage piping underground, even if it's only the sewer service line. Many houses with basements and all slab-on-grade homes will have soil pipes trenched in place before the concrete goes down. If you build an addition that requires below-grade piping or if you break out some portion of your existing concrete to add piping, you'll need to know the basics.

In-ground piping must be able to support the substantial weight of the soil and concrete above it. This means that the trench you dig for the pipe must be uniform, with adequate slope, and without extreme high spots or voids. High spots can squeeze a pipe out of round, hindering flow. Voids beneath the pipe can cause sags and breaks.

When you install in-ground piping, take all the time you need to perfect the trench bed. Use a level on each length of pipe to ensure adequate slope. As always, shoot for ¼ inch of slope per foot. Dig as deep as you must to meet an existing pipe or sewer service line. In the case of a new home, this may mean digging under an exterior footing. In a remodel, dig to the same level as the pipe into which you need to splice. Always try to square the sides of the trench. A 12- to 16-inch width is ideal, but try not to overexcavate. If you happen to dig too deeply, don't try to undo your mistake by packing soil back into the trench. Disturbed soil will continue to settle for years. Bring a low spot back to grade with compactible sand or gravel. Sand is really the best way to ensure a uniform trench.

Protect the Piping. If careless concrete workers are likely to bump into floor drains, laundry stands, and stack risers and leave them permanently out of position, stake these fittings in place with ½-inch iron rebar topped with a pipe holder. This will keep the pipes stable and help them resist any inadvertent manhandling. Also, be sure to cover the top of each riser and floor-drain screen with duct tape when you're finished installing the pipe. This will keep concrete and other debris from falling into them. Many a homeowner has had to jackhammer the floor of a spanking-new home to retrieve a chunk of construction debris from the soil pipe. If you're installing a toilet in the addition, cover the top of the toilet drain with a plastic cap before the concrete goes down.

Providing Cleanout Access. Codes stipulate that each drain stack must have a permanently accessible cleanout fitting at its base. (Dry-vent stacks don't need cleanouts.) Where you have reduced a 4-inch soil pipe to a 3-inch stack, make the cleanout T-fitting the size of the larger pipe. If the stack is more than 10 feet from the wall, codes require an additional cleanout fitting. You can place this cleanout just inside the wall, in the basement floor, or just outside the house, brought to grade. If you'll be finishing that area of the basement, an exterior cleanout fitting is practical. And, finally, most codes require additional cleanout fittings in above-grade kitchen lines. Install one after a change of direction.

Installing In-Ground Drainpipes

1 Dig the soil-pipe trench at a slight downward slope, and tunnel a minimum of 20 in. under the basement footing.

2 Install the first length of cast-iron pipe under the footing, and use a spirit level to check that its slope is adequate.

3 Drive a stake clamp next to the toilet riser and stack fittings to hold them in place until the concrete is poured.

4 Cover the tops of all floor drains and stacks using tape to keep construction debris from falling into the piping system.

5 Instead of sealing it with tape, install a plastic closet cap over the toilet riser. The concrete floor will be poured around this cap.

How to Cut Cast Iron

You have a choice of methods when cutting cast-iron pipe. While a hacksaw will work, it's a tedious process and sometimes requires several blades per cut. When professionals cut cast iron, they use a snap-cutter. As its name implies, this tool doesn't saw through, but snaps—breaks—a pipe in two. A snap-cutter consists of a roller chain that has hardened steel wheels built into it, spaced an inch apart. The chain is connected to a ratchet or scissor head. As you lever the head, the chain tightens, and the cutter wheels bite into the pipe with equal pressure. When you apply enough pressure, the pipe snaps in two. Snap-cutters are common rental items.

Another cutting method is to repeatedly score the pipe with a ball-peen hammer and cold chisel. This method is slow and requires access to the entire circumference of the pipe, but it works surprisingly well. To cut cast-iron pipe with a cold chisel, draw a line completely around the pipe at the appropriate spot using chalk or a grease pencil. Then strike the chisel along this line until you've made it completely around the pipe. Repeat the rotation until the pipe breaks apart. As you tap—usually five to seven rotations—the chisel weakens the cast along the line and eventually breaks it more or less evenly.

If the pipe breaks unevenly, you can break off any high spots using an old adjustable wrench. Just grip about ¼ inch of pipe with the jaws of the wrench, and strike the handle. With several strikes, you'll chip away enough material to even the edge.

Choosing a Method. Which method is best? It all depends on the location of the pipe and the amount of room in which you have to work. When installing new piping or cutting into an existing line underneath the basement floor, a snap-cutter is quick and easy. But if the pipe rests against a wall, a cutter chain may not fit between the wall and pipe. This pipe position would also prohibit the cold-chisel approach. In this case, a hacksaw is your best choice.

Cutting Cast Iron with a Chisel

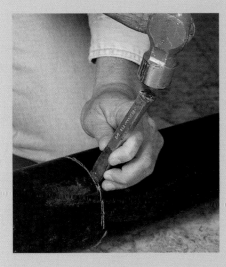

1 Draw a line around the pipe, and score along this line until the pipe breaks in two.

2 If the cut leaves any unevenness, break off the high spots using an old adjustable wrench.

A rented snap-cutter makes cutting cast-iron drainpipes quick and easy.

Making Lead-and-Oakum Joints

Use a packing tool to tamp the joint two-thirds full of oakum.

Cap the oakum with lead wool, and tamp it into solid packing.

Joining Cast-Iron Pipe

1 To install a gasket, reach through and roll half of it up. Press the other half into the hub and release.

2 Lubricate the gasket with soap.

3 Use a shovel to force the pipe through it. You should hear the pipe bottom out.

4 Install a Y-fitting in a fashion similar to that for the hub connections, and then rotate it into position for the branch line.

Connections with Neoprene Fittings

Use banded couplings to splice plastic piping into a cast-iron drainage line.

Install a no-hub flexible fitting for greater ease in retrofitting drainpipes.

Working with Plastic Drainpipe

PVC (and ABS) pipes and fittings, once cemented together, stay that way. Unlike wood glues, which bind each piece of wood to itself, plastic pipe solvents actually melt one surface into the other, creating a chemical weld. With a 1½-inch pipe and fitting, you'll have about 30 seconds to change your mind about the joint. After that, it's permanent. So test-fit and mark each group of fittings with a pencil or felt-tip marker before gluing them in place.

When measuring for a pipe cut, be sure to include the depth of the fitting hubs in your total. You can make this calculation in your head, but holding an actual fitting in place helps to eliminate errors. When you've determined the exact pipe length needed, mark the pipe and cut it. You can use a hacksaw, handsaw (with miter box), PVC saw, wheel cutter, or power miter saw (cutoff saw). Be careful to keep the cut square, because an angled pipe won't fit as well into the fitting. And when cutting, make long, easy strokes. Moving the saw too fast can cause the saw blade to overheat, gumming it up and leaving hard-to-remove burrs in the pipe.

Smooth the inside of the pipe end using a knife, sandpaper, or a deburring tool before cementing the joint together. Any rough edges will attract hair and strands of fabric sent though the drainage system, causing clogs, and in some cases, depleting a trap seal through capillary attraction.

With the end of the pipe cleared of burrs and rough spots, apply primer-solvent to the outer edge of the pipe and to the hub of the fitting. Both primer-solvent and joint-cement containers come with applicators. When the primer evaporates, test-fit the joints, making sure that the pipe bottoms out in the fittings. When you're sure the joint is right, mark the pipe to show where the fitting should land on it in final assembly. Next, coat the first 1 inch of the pipe and the entire inside of the fitting hub with cement. Immediately insert the pipe and fitting. As soon as the pipe bottoms out in the hub, rotate the fitting about one-quarter turn. This fills any voids in the joint by breaking up the insertion lines. Of course, if you've test-fitted your joints first, you'll need to push the pipe into the fitting with the alignment marks about one-quarter turn out of sync, then rotate the fitting until the marks line up. Hold the parts together for about 10 seconds. Wipe any excess cement from the outside of the pipe or fitting. Complete the assembly with any additional pipes or fittings.

Working with Plastic Drainpipe

1 Measure the pipe using a measuring tape. Don't forget to allow extra length to extend into the fitting's hub.

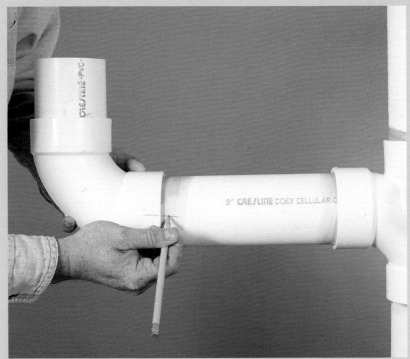

5 Test-fit the assembly, and mark each joint for alignment with a pencil. You could also number the pieces.

2 Cut the pipe (here, with a hacksaw). You can also use a handsaw, special PVC saw, wheel cutter, or power miter saw.

3 Use an inexpensive deburring tool or the rounded side of a file to smooth the ragged edge left by the saw.

4 Apply primer to the end of the pipe to cut the glaze. Many primers have an added colorant. Primer is often code required.

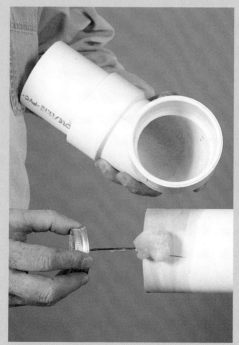

6 Apply PVC solvent cement using the applicator contained in the can. Cover both the pipe ends and the inside of each hub.

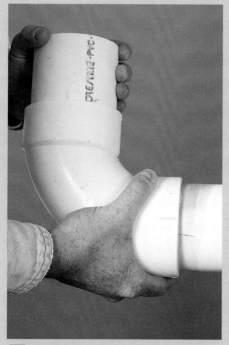

7 Start the fitting slightly out of alignment, and rotate it to line up the marks. This breaks up the insertion lines of the glue.

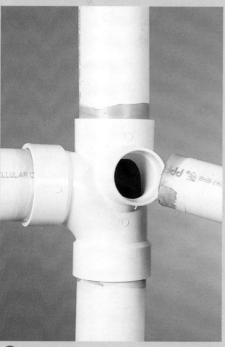

8 Install the stack fittings first, then the branch lines. A side-inlet T-fitting (shown) can drain both toilet and shower.

water pipes

Pipe Basics

Water piping is easier to install than waste and vent piping in many respects, and it's certainly easier to design. With no gravity or venting issues to worry about, size and efficiency become the focus.

Size is relatively easy to determine. A ½-inch line can serve only two fixtures, so in almost all cases you'll run water supply trunk lines in ¾-inch pipe until you reach the last two fixtures, and then reduce to ½-inch piping. (Sizes always indicate the inside diameter of the pipe.) The same sizing rule applies to branch lines extending from the main trunk lines. (See Chapter 1, "Making Plans," starting on page 15, for more specific information on system design and code requirements.)

If you do the job neatly, using no more pipe than necessary, you'll have an efficient system. If you anchor all in-wall stub-outs and valves, support the pipe every few feet, and protect it from freezing, you can expect decades of trouble-free service. And if you insulate the hot-water lines, you'll save on water-heating costs.

One drawback might be the water-pipe joining method. Water pipes are usually made of copper, which must be soldered. Well soldered joints require some skill, but with practice and the information in this chapter, good soldering technique is not beyond your reach.

Of course, you might worry about leaks, but leaks are fairly easy to repair. Just drain the system, and redo the offending fitting. It may be inconvenient and time-consuming, but it's not difficult.

Cutting Water Pipes

The methods and equipment you need to cut water pipes depend on the piping material itself. Many people cut copper and galvanized steel using a hacksaw, but a tubing cutter leaves a more uniform edge. You can also cut plastic pipe using a tubing cutter, but most do-it-yourselfers reach for a hacksaw instead. The reason has less to do with the quality of the cut than with the availability of the tool. Tubing shears are probably the best cutting tool for plastic types of pipe.

A clean, straight cut is also important. A tubing cutter can leave a compression ridge inside the pipe, while hacksaws leave coarse burrs. Ragged burrs protruding from a pipe's edge will eventually break off and make their way into control valves, appliances, and faucets. Severe edges also create friction in the water flow, called line friction, which can reduce pressure. And finally, raised edges generate turbulence, which can eventually erode the pipe wall. To prevent these problems, ream any severe edges left by a cutting tool before you install the pipe.

To ream a copper or plastic pipe, lift the triangular reaming attachment from the top of the cutter, insert it into the end of the pipe, and give it several sharp twists. When dealing with steel pipe, you'll need a more aggressive reaming tool—one with hardened-steel cutting blades. If you rent other tools to work with steel pipe (such as a threader), rent a reamer as well. If you are making only a few cuts, use a rat-tail file.

Safe Soldering

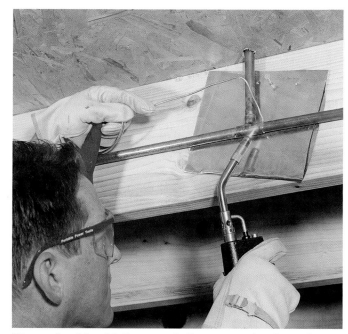

Use a double thickness of sheet metal to keep from scorching the wood.

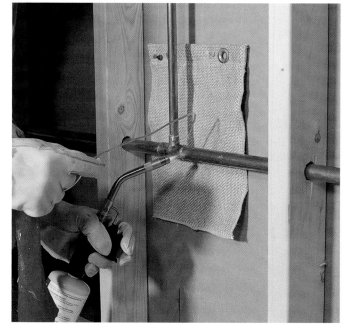

You can also use a flame shield of fireproof woven fabric to protect larger areas.

Copper Water Piping

Copper pipe is available in two forms—*rigid*, or hard, and *drawn*, or soft. Rigid copper comes in 10- or 20-foot lengths, while soft copper comes in 60-, 100-, and 120-foot coils. You typically use rigid copper for in-house, above-concrete water-piping installations, and soft copper for belowground applications and for connecting stub-outs with faucets. Along with black steel pipe, some codes allow soft copper for both natural gas and propane piping installations.

Rigid copper is available in Type M and Type L wall thicknesses. Type M, thinner than Type L, is used predominantly in residential systems. Type L is more common in commercial installations. Soft copper comes in Type L and Type K wall thicknesses—Type K is heavier. You use Type L most often aboveground, as both water and gas piping, while you use Type K almost exclusively for underground water piping. Type K soft copper is also used to run water service lines between public mains and private homes.

You can join rigid copper with soldered—or sweat—fittings, compression fittings, and push-fit fittings. You can join soft copper with compression and flare fittings. Threaded adapters are available for joining copper to any other threaded material, including threaded steel and CPVC plastic. Only soldered and threaded fittings can be hidden in walls, however.

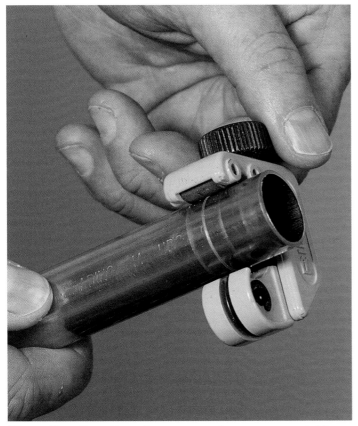

Use a thumb cutter when you need to cut copper tubing and you're confined by a tight working space.

Using a Tubing Cutter

Use all tubing cutters in a similar fashion. First, mark the pipe to length. Then clamp the cutter onto the pipe, centering the cutting wheel on your mark. Rotate the tool's handle clockwise until the cutting wheel bites into the pipe just a little. Don't overdo it. If it's difficult to rotate the cutter around the pipe, unscrew the handle, but just slightly. Rotate the tool around the pipe several times. You'll feel slight resistance on the first one or two turns, but after that, the cutter will roll easily around the pipe. This is your cue to tighten the wheel against the pipe again. Rotate the cutter, and repeat this procedure until you cut all the way through the pipe.

You use the same method for cutting plastic, steel, or copper. The only difference is that tubing cutters made for steel pipe are much heavier than those for copper and plastic. Because of this, there's a substantial cost difference. Buying a tubing cutter for plastic and copper makes sense—one will work for both—but cutters made for steel pipe are strictly rental items. In fact, if you have only one or two cuts to make, you should probably have your local hardware store or plumbing supply center cut and thread the pipes for you.

Thumb Cutter. You'll find a variety of tubing cutters on the market, most having an overall length of 5 to 6 inches. These do well in the open, but when working in walls and between joists, a close-quarters tubing cutter—sometimes called a *thumb cutter*—is often a better choice. Instead of a long handle, a thumb cutter has a knurled knob. The tool works surprisingly well, and some models handle pipes up to 1 inch in diameter. If you can afford only one tubing cutter for copper pipe, a thumb cutter is a good choice. It'll slow you down a little, but you'll be able to use it in more places.

Cutting with a Hacksaw

Use as much of the blade as possible in long, easy strokes. If you work too fast, the blade will heat up and start binding. A hot blade also leaves a ragged pipe edge. The best approach is to steady the pipe on a solid surface and cut just to the left or right of the support. Some people like to use a miter box to ensure straight cuts.

Close-Quarters Hacksaws. When you need a smaller saw, you'll find that there are a variety of miniature hacksaws on the market. While it's not sensible to try plumbing an entire job with a tiny saw, they work wonders in cramped spaces. In fact, close-quarters hacksaws often work in situations too cramped for thumb cutters. The design shown in the photo opposite right is usually preferable. In a pinch, some people remove the blade from a full-size hacksaw and use it alone. But hacksaw blades are fairly brittle, so remember to wear gloves.

Solder

Solder is metallic filler that bonds two metallic surfaces to itself. Flux helps this bonding to occur. Flux works by ridding the copper surfaces of oxidation and other contaminants. It pulls molten solder into the joint, even when the fitting is upside down. Where the flux goes, solder will follow. Without flux, molten solder will just bead up and fall away.

Until the 1980s, most of the solder used in residential plumbing was a 50-50 amalgamation of tin and lead. Other combinations included 60-40 and 95-5 tin and lead. Lead was almost always an ingredient. The industry used lead solder because it was a familiar product in sheet-metal work when copper pipe became popular after World War II. Lead

melts at relatively low temperatures and bridges gaps well, so it's easier to use than other kinds of solders, which are harder. Lead also makes brass more easily machined, so most quality faucets contained lead until very recently.

The plumbing industry didn't realize that water, under fairly common conditions, could leach lead from soldered fittings. Even small amounts of lead ingested by a human being can cause brain damage. Today, the U.S. Environmental Protection Agency (EPA) bans the use of lead-based plumbing solder.

Using a Tubing Cutter

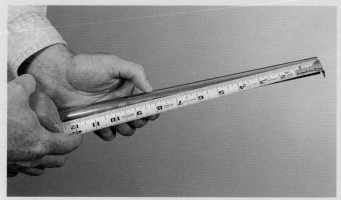

1 Hold the pipe in your left hand and the measuring tape in your right. Hold the location with your thumb; then mark it using a pencil.

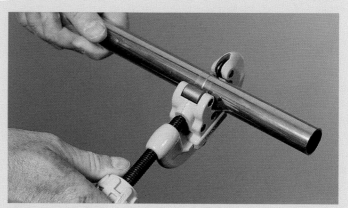

2 Tighten the wheel cutter to clamp it onto the pipe at the mark, and rotate the cutter with the wheel following the rollers.

Using Hacksaws

Use a fine-tooth blade in a hacksaw. Hold the pipe steady, cutting near the support.

You can use a miniature hacksaw as you would a full-size one, but it fits in tight spaces.

Soldering Copper Tubing

To begin, clean both the pipe ends and the fitting ports. The best approach is to sand them using grit cloth, fine sandpaper, an abrasive scouring pad, or a wire brush. Wire brushes for cleaning fittings are available at plumbing outlets. Many people get good results from using a wire brush for fittings and an abrasive pad for pipes. Sand each pipe at least 1 inch up from its end, even if the pipe is shiny and new. New pipes and fittings still need sanding because they may have a coating of oil or other substance.

After you have sanded the pipe and fitting and wiped them clean, use a small brush to apply a thin coating of flux to the pipe end as well as to the inner surface of the fitting. Insert each pipe into its fitting hub fully, and wipe away the excess flux. (If you're soldering an assembly that spans more than one joist or stud, secure the pipe to the structural framing using pipe clamps or hangers, as necessary, as you assemble the fittings. To save time, it pays to assemble a group of fittings, and then to solder them all in sequence, from the bottom up.) Once you start soldering a fitting, solder all the hubs on that fitting before moving on. Try to solder all the assembled fittings within 30 minutes, because some brands of flux will degrade the copper if they're left on the pipe or fitting surface longer.

When you have a group of pipes and fittings assembled, wrap a couple of feet of solder wire around your hand to form an oval-shaped spool. Remove the spool from your hand, and pull one end out roughly 10 inches. Then bend down the final 2 inches of this length into a 90-degree angle. This makes a convenient roll of wire that you can spool out as needed. The 90-degree bend allows you to comfortably approach the fitting from nearly any direction.

When you are going to heat a brass valve, it's a good idea to remove the cartridge or stem. This simple precaution helps to avoid warping the nylon and neoprene components. If you decide not to take the valve apart, at least turn the valve to its fully open position. Then angle the torch tip away from the valve body, and heat only the valve's hubs. In any case, try to keep the flame from hitting the copper pipes directly. Copper heats faster than brass.

Before lighting the torch, gather everything you'll need, including the torch, solder, wiping rag, job light (if needed), ladder, and flux. Keep the flux nearby in case you inadvertently scorch a fitting. With everything ready, light the torch and turn the valve wide open. If you're right-handed, place the torch in your left hand and the solder and rag in your right. Heat the most accessible side of the lowest hub on the first fitting, moving the flame in an arc across the front half of the hub.

As soon as the lower hub of the fitting takes, heat the next-highest hub and repeat the procedure. Keep in mind that the fitting is already quite hot, so it takes only a few seconds of heat on the remaining hubs. To avoid overheating, keep touching the solder to the joint. When you've finished soldering all hubs on the fitting and before the solder hardens, use your rag to carefully wipe away the excess.

Soldering Copper Tubing

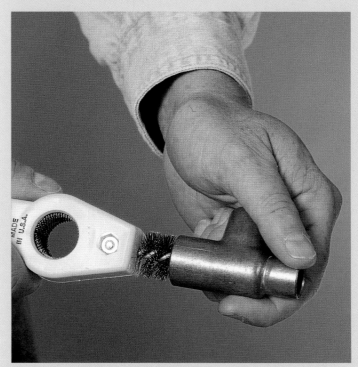

1 Use a combination tool, wire brush, or abrasive pad to clean each hub on the fitting. Combination tools have two different brush sizes.

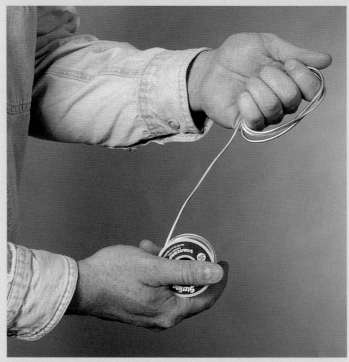

4 Pull approximately 24 in. of solder from the spool, and wrap it around your hand for a more comfortable grip.

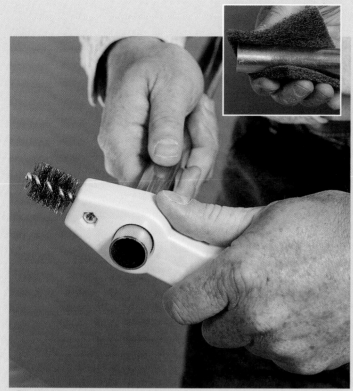

2 Scour the end of each pipe until it's shiny at least 1 in. back where the fitting will be attached. Wipe the pipe and fitting with a rag (inset).

3 Apply flux to the pipe end and the inside of the fitting with a small brush. Insert the pipe, and wipe away the excess flux.

5 To keep from scorching the rubber and plastic parts in a shutoff valve, remove the stem before soldering the valve.

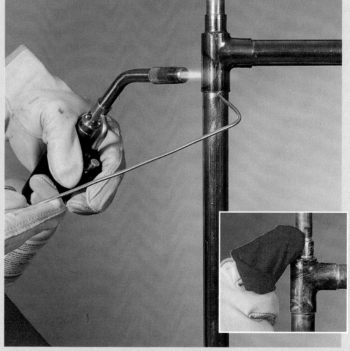

6 Heat the lowest hub on the fitting. Touch the solder to the fitting. Continue to heat the fitting until the solder melts. When you've finished and before the solder hardens, wipe the excess solder from each joint (inset).

Installing Compression Fittings

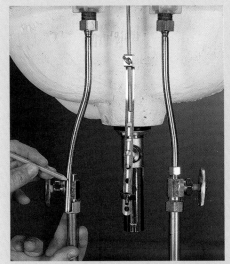 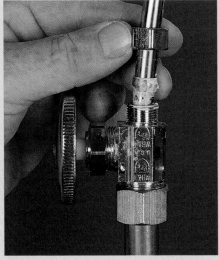 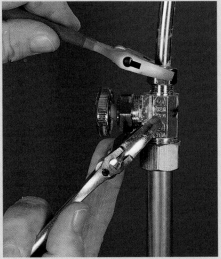

1 Bend the supply tube into shape using a tubing bender; test-fit it; and mark the length. Cut the tube, and slide the compression nut and ferrule onto its end.

2 Coat the ferrule and threads with pipe joint compound; insert the tube into the compression fitting; and slide the ferrule and nut down. Tighten the nut finger-tight.

3 Backhold the valve with one 6-in. adjustable wrench, and tighten the top compression nut with another. Turn the nut only about 1½ turns.

Compression Fittings

A compression-type water fitting consists of a brass body—either an adapter body or valve body—with two or more pipe hubs. The fitting hubs have external threads and beveled rims. The nuts are open at the top so that you can insert pipes through them. A third component, a brass compression ring called a ferrule, makes the seal. The ferrule is also beveled, top and bottom.

You make the connection by sliding the nut and ferrule onto the end of a pipe and inserting the pipe into the fitting hub. As you tighten the nut, the beveled surfaces force the ring inward, cinching it around the pipe. The ring crushes the pipe a little, making a water seal. The problem comes in not knowing how much to tighten the compression nut. If you overtighten it, you can reduce the ring too much, and water will seep past the nut. When you see a leak, your first impulse is to tighten the nut even more. But in this case, tightening just widens the gap and makes the leak worse. At this point, there's no chance of saving the connection. Your only option is to start over, using a new supply tube and ring.

You most frequently use compression fittings as conversion fittings under fixtures. Used in this way, they join rigid copper supply lines to flexible copper supply tubes. Compression-type connectors normally come with shutoff valves, but they're also available as couplings and 90-degree L-fittings, in sizes ranging from ⅛ to 1 inch in diameter. You can also find valves and adapters with one threaded hub and one compression hub. Use these to join threaded brass water fittings to copper supply tubes.

Installing Compression Fittings. If the alignment between faucet and riser requires an offset, begin by bending the supply tube to meet the fittings head-on. Use a tubing bender so that you don't crimp the soft copper tubing as you shape it. Then hold or temporarily fasten the supply tube in place, and mark it for length. Trim the tube, making sure that any bends are well away from its end. Bending a pipe forces it out of round, preventing the nut and ring from sliding on.

Once the supply tube is ready, slide the nut and ferrule onto it an inch or two, and lubricate both the ring and fitting threads with a thin coating of pipe joint compound. Insert the pipe into the fitting port; slide the compression ring down to meet the fitting; and thread the nut onto the fitting finger-tight. When the connection feels snug, use a 6-inch adjustable wrench to tighten the nut 1½ turns.

Compression Fittings

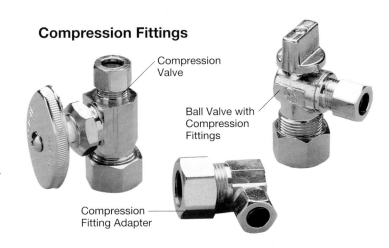

Compression Valve

Ball Valve with Compression Fittings

Compression Fitting Adapter

Making Flare-Fitting Connections

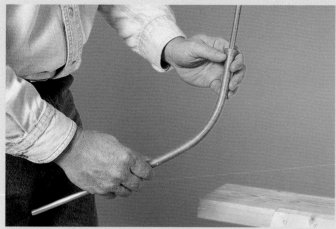

1 Use a spring-type tubing bender to avoid kinking soft copper tubes. These work on both copper and chrome-plated supply tubes.

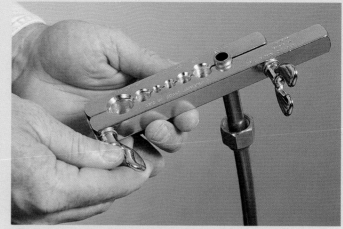

2 With a clamp-type flaring tool, clamp the base onto the pipe with about ⅛ in. of pipe showing above the top surface of the base.

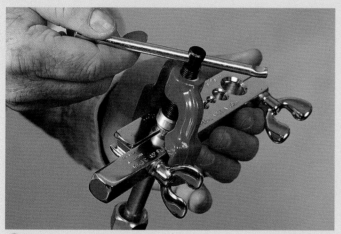

3 Make sure the stem will clear the pipe, and slide the flaring vise on from one end. Thread the head down into the pipe opening.

4 Continue threading the tool into the pipe until the rim becomes flared out about 1/16 in. Getting the right flare might take some trial and error.

5 Apply a light coating of pipe joint compound to the male end of the flare fitting, and screw it into place.

6 Coat the free end of the flare fitting with pipe joint compound. Thread the nut onto the fitting until it is finger-tight (inset). Tighten using two wrenches.

Steel Piping

Galvanized and black steel are the two types of steel pipe used in residential plumbing. You can install galvanized steel as water or gas pipe. However, use black steel, where allowed, only as gas pipe. Don't be tempted to use black steel in your plumbing system. The use of black steel for water is prohibited by many codes because water causes black steel to rust quickly.

Aside from their separate uses, there's little difference in how the two are cut and fitted. You can cut both types of steel with a heavy wheel cutter or a hacksaw and use threaded fittings on both. You can purchase short, threaded nipples at any hardware store, but you'll need to rent threading dies to cut threads on custom lengths. While few people use either type today, there is plenty of it in place, and you may need to know something about it to make repairs and additions.

Cutting, Threading, and Fitting Steel Pipe

1 Clamp the pipe in the vise, and clamp the wheel cutter onto the pipe. Tighten and rotate the cutter.

2 Cut any inside burr from the pipe using a heavy-duty reaming tool. Stop when you no longer feel the burr.

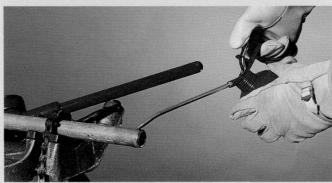

3 Apply oil to the pipe end.

4 Slide the threading die onto the pipe. While applying pressure, slowly crank the tool clockwise.

5 Spread pipe joint compound over the newly cut male threads, using the applicator brush that comes with the container.

6 Use a pipe wrench to tighten the fitting onto the pipe. Tighten until it feels snug. Use a nipple in the fitting (right) to preserve the threads.

Plastic Water Piping

Plastic water pipe, made of chlorinated polyvinyl chloride (CPVC), has been around for years, and when properly installed, has proved to be durable. Its appeal, of course, is its ease of installation. CPVC piping can be installed with the most common of household tools and by people with almost no previous experience. The problem is that some plumbing codes have not come up to speed on CPVC as a potable water carrier.

Electrical Grounding and Plastic. Few homeowners understand the relationship between a home's plumbing and electrical systems. In many jurisdictions, the electrical panel is grounded through metallic water piping. Because the metallic piping inside the house connects to a metallic water service pipe that is buried underground, most codes require that the electrical system use this piping for all or part of its path to ground in order to have a safe installation.

If you cut out a section of cold-water trunk line and splice a length of plastic piping in its place, there's a good chance that you'll interrupt this path to ground. That's a dangerous situation. If you decide to splice plastic into a cold-water trunk line, install a heavy grounding conductor across the span. This jumper wire should be the same size as the service panel's existing grounding wire, usually 6 gauge. Attach the wire to the metallic pipes using code-approved grounding clamps, one on each side of the splice. You won't need a jumper where the grounding wire connects directly to the water service pipe on the street side of the meter.

To insulate existing pipes using foam insulation, open the seam and tape the insulation in place.

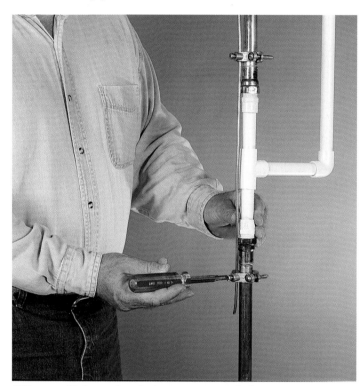

When splicing plastic into copper piping, you may need to install a copper jumper wire to maintain an unbroken ground for the home's wiring system.

CPVC versus Copper

Is CPVC plastic as good as copper for common residential plumbing applications? In most cases, yes. But this is true only if it is not used underground or under concrete, if it has no chance to freeze, and when the installation is made according to manufacturer's specifications and is code-worthy. In some cases—for example, in cabins and second homes where water can stand long enough to corrode copper—plastic may actually be the best choice.

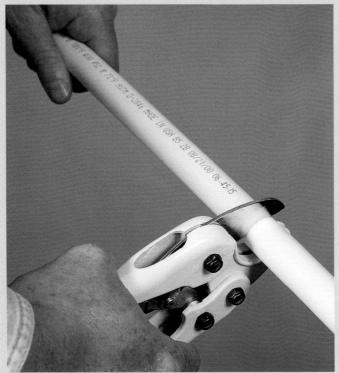

1 Use plastic-pipe-cutting shears to cut CPVC. Be sure to allow for the depth of the fitting hub. This tool makes the cleanest possible cut.

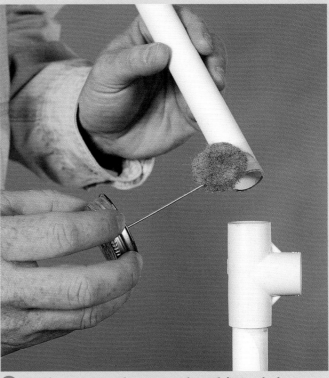

2 Apply primer to the pipe ends and fitting hubs. Primer removes the surface glaze and reduces leaks. Use sandpaper if you don't have primer.

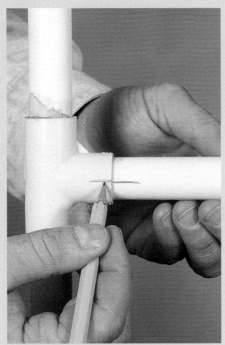

3 Test-fit the pipe and fittings. Before you disassemble the pipe and cement it, mark the final alignment with a pencil.

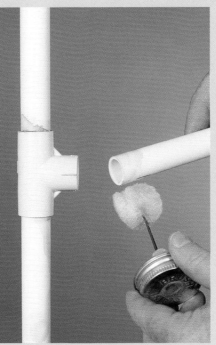

4 Apply CPVC solvent cement to the pipe and fitting hub, and insert the pipe about one-quarter turn out of alignment.

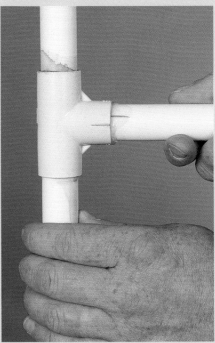

5 Rotate the pipe one-quarter turn after inserting it to line up the pencil marks. This spreads the cement and accelerates curing.

Cutting and Fitting CPVC Pipe

CPVC piping comes in a variety of diameters: ⅜, ½, ¾, and 1 inch. The fitting assortment made for other kinds of piping is also available in CPVC. The best way to cut it is using special shears. These cutters slice the plastic cleanly, leaving almost no ridges or ragged edges. Like the PVC made for drainpipes, CPVC comes with a surface glaze that you must remove before you cement it. If you leave this glaze in place, you increase the chances of a leak. The best remover is a solvent-primer, which comes in containers with lid-mounted applicators. Dab primer on the pipe area to be cemented. Do the same to the inner surfaces of the fitting hubs. Allow the primer to evaporate before making the joint. You can also cut the glaze by scuffing the final 1 inch of the pipe and the inner surfaces of each fitting hub.

After you remove the surface glaze, test-fit the joints you want to make. Make alignment marks on the fitting and the pipe using a pencil or marker. You'll use these marks later to line up the pipes and fittings in exactly the same positions when you rotate the parts as you put them together. Apply a thin but even coating of joint solvent cement inside the hub of the fitting and to the outside of the pipe, using the container's applicator. Insert the pipe into the fitting, and rotate it one-quarter turn, using the alignment marks you made previously as a guide. Rotating the pipe or fitting helps fill any voids in the cement and creates friction, which serves to accelerate the chemical bonding slightly. As with PVC drainpipe, once you have cemented the joint you'll have very little time to change your mind. If you find that you've made a mistake, pull the joint apart immediately. Then you can apply new solvent cement and remake the joint.

Other Plastic Pipe

Polybutylene pipe was used a good deal in the 1970s and '80s, but it is no longer on the market. There is plenty of it still in place, however. If you come across this flexible gray plastic pipe in a residential water system, you can make repairs using copper or CPVC and transition fittings.

A more popular plastic pipe these days is cross-linked polyethylene (PEX). It's available in a variety of colors, including red, black, white, blue, and clear. Unlike other plastic piping on the market, PEX is now routinely installed by professional plumbers and is code compliant in many areas of the country, though certainly not all. It is a high-quality material that is used extensively in the Southwest, where acidic water and soil eat through copper pipes. It is also used almost exclusively in radiant-floor applications, in which hot water is run through concrete floor slabs to warm the floor and heat the home. You'll most often find it in wholesale plumbing supply stores.

You can join PEX pipes using crimp-ring fittings, but codes allow these fittings only in exposed installations. For code-worthy in-wall installations, you'll need barbed fittings made especially for PEX tubing. Unfortunately, these fittings are proprietary and require special tools not readily available to homeowners.

PEX pipe uses threaded barbed adapters to connect to valves. Install the fitting, and slide the pipe onto the barb.

To lock the PEX pipe onto a barbed fitting, plumbers use a proprietary crimp-ring tool.

chapter 4

toilets

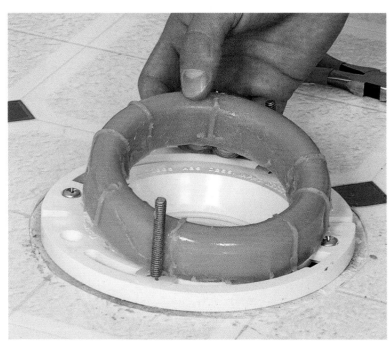

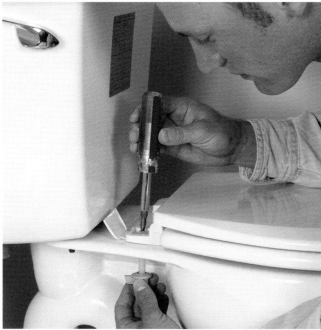

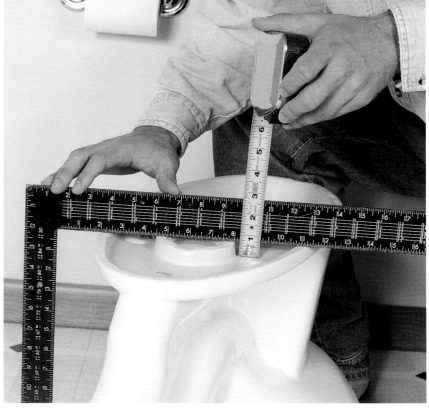

Toilet Fundamentals

Water-flush toilets are miracles of simplicity. In fact, few devices accomplish as much with so few parts. They're so simply built that you can completely overhaul one in about an hour, for about $20 in parts. The latest generation of water-savers may be a little more complicated, but repairing them is work you can still do.

Water-powered toilets come in two forms, gravity-flow and pressure-assisted models. Gravity-flow toilets use only the force of gravity to flush wastewater. Pressure-assisted models use the extra power of compressed air to push water more forcefully. The basic waste-removal system is similar in both types. Water flows into the tank via the fill valve. When you flush the toilet, the water flows through the flush valve, into and through the bowl, and through the trap, taking waste with it. Knowing this sequence will later help you match symptoms with solutions.

How Gravity-Flow Toilets Work

When you press down on the flush handle, its lever lifts a chain or lift wire attached to a flapper or tank ball. (Flappers have chains; tank balls have lift wires.) The chain or wire lifts the flapper or ball from its flush-valve seat, which allows water to escape through the valve.

Both flappers and tank balls are hollow. Some are open at the bottom, and some are closed, but both drain water and trap air, making them temporarily buoyant when you push down on the handle. Without this buoyancy, the flapper or ball would sink immediately, so you'd need to hold the flush lever down until the tank was empty.

As the flushing water recedes, the flapper or ball floats downward until it rests in the flush-valve seat and stops up the opening. Once seated, it is flooded with water and held down by the weight of the water rising above it.

After passing through the flush valve, the water from the tank travels in two directions. Much of it shoots through the siphon jet, the small opening across from the trap outlet. The rest flows to the hollow rim around the top of the bowl, where it spills through slanted holes in the underside of the rim.

The water rushing in through the siphon jet overflows the trap, priming it. Once primed, the trap siphons all the water it can over its weir, or crown, stopping only when there's not enough water in the bowl to sustain the siphon. At this point, all water on the house side of the trap slides back into the bowl.

Because the rim holes are slanted, the water entering the bowl through the rim travels diagonally around the bowl. This diagonal pattern scours the sides of the bowl, but it also sends the water over the trap in a spiraling motion, which improves the efficiency of the flush.

Replacing a Flush Handle

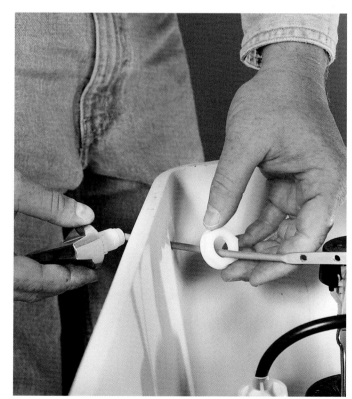

Remove the nut from the old lever, and pull the lever through the tank hole.

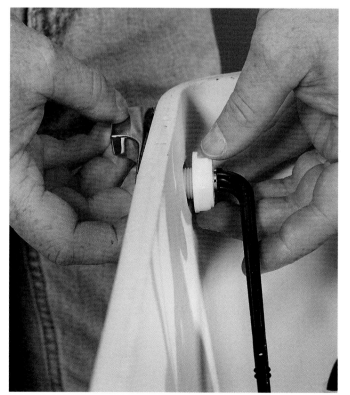

Slide the new lever in place, and tighten the nut. The nut has left-hand threads.

As the bowl empties, new water enters the tank through the ballcock or fill valve. (All ballcocks are fill valves, but not all fill valves are ballcocks. The term "ballcock" applies only to traditional fill valves, which have ball floats on the end of a pivoting arm. Newer fill valves use a vertically mounted float cup.) This flow begins the moment you flush the toilet. Most of the water entering the tank does so through a tube that terminates near the bottom of the tank. Delivering the water to the bottom of the tank provides a measure of noise control. The sound is muffled as soon as the water in the tank rises above the end of the tube. At the same time, a small stream of water is diverted into the flush valve overflow tube—via a ⅛-inch-diameter fill tube—and falls directly into the bowl's rim. This stream restores the water in the bowl to its maximum level. As soon as the tank fills, the float shuts off the fill valve, and the toilet is ready for another flush.

Water-Saving Toilets

Responding to legislation enacted several years ago, manufacturers reduced the volume of water needed to flush a toilet efficiently. Ironically, the very first toilets had small flush tanks, holding only about 3 gallons. These toilets worked because the tanks were mounted on the wall, high above the bowl. Elevating water in a column increases its downward force—an effect known as head pressure. The more pressure generated for the flush, the less water you need. The reverse is also true, so when tanks were moved down the wall and mounted on or just above the bowl, manufacturers increased the size of the tanks to as much as 8 gallons. This was clearly more volume than was needed, and the industry eventually settled on 5 gallons.

During the late 1960s and into the '70s, fresh water came to be recognized as a limited resource, and tank size was reduced again, to 3.5 gallons.

Gravity-Flow Toilet Anatomy

Fill-Valve Assembly

Float
Float Lift Wire
Water Inlet
Gasket
Coupling Nut
Supply Line
Shutoff Valve
Weir
Trap
Toilet Flange
To Stack
Hold-Down Bolt

Tank

Flush-Valve Assembly

Fill Tube
Overflow Tube
Flapper
Tank Mounting Bolt
Spud Nut
Spud Washer
Spiral Water Flow from Rim Holes
Seat Mounting Hole

Bowl

Siphon Jet Tube
Water from siphon jet opening "jump starts" flushing process.
Wax Ring
Closet Bend

Water-Savers Are the Law.

In the late 1970s, a number of Scandinavian countries began using—and mandating—super-low-flow toilets, which flushed with an amazingly skimpy 1.6 gallons of water. Before long, these toilets appeared at trade shows here in the United States, and manufacturers began experimenting with low-flow toilets, trying to improve performance. Eventually, the U.S. enacted a national standard that limits to 1.6 gallons per flush (gpf) the water used by residential toilets made in this country after January 1, 1994.

Do low-flow toilets work as well as 3.5-gpf ones? The early models certainly didn't. From the start, manufacturers offered two distinctly different low-flow toilets; a gravity-flow model and a pressure-assisted model. The gravity-flow models were like traditional toilets but with minor changes all around, including new fill valves and flush valves. Engineers reduced trap geometry, along with water spots—the surface area of the bowl water—and outlet diameters to cut down the flow of water. These early water misers were so sluggish that

1.6-Gallon Gravity-Flow Toilet

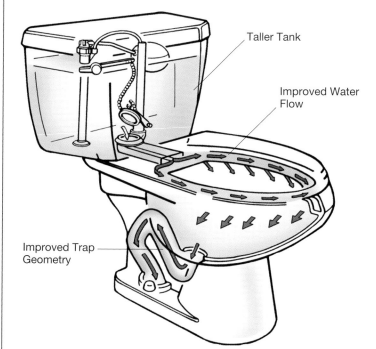

Taller Tank

Improved Water Flow

Improved Trap Geometry

Pressure-Assisted Toilet

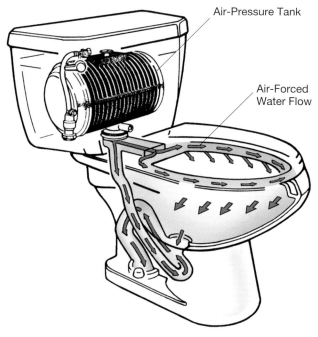

Air-Pressure Tank

Air-Forced Water Flow

they often needed additional flushes to clear and clean the bowl, and clogs were common. With steady engineering refinements, however, gravity-flow toilets now work reasonably well and are a good choice for most households.

Pressure-Assisted Toilets. In general, pressure-assisted toilets work better than gravity models. These toilets use incoming water to compress air in a chamber inside the tank. (A water pressure of at least 20 pounds per square inch is required.) Flushing releases this compressed air in a burst, forcing water to prime the trap almost instantly. Air assist allows the tank to operate with less water, making more water available for the bowl. More water in the bowl means a larger water spot and a cleaner bowl. And finally, the tank-within-a-tank construction completely eliminates tank sweat caused by condensation during hot, humid weather.

With these advantages, you'd think everyone would want a pressure-assisted toilet, but that hasn't been the case. The most common complaints are that they're too noisy and too complicated. Starting each flush with a burst of compressed air does make them noisy, and they're certainly less familiar. Most people would recognize the tank components in a traditional toilet, but lift the lid on a pressure-assisted unit, and all you'll see is a sealed plastic drum, a water-inlet mechanism, a hose, and a flush cartridge. Most manufacturers use almost identical tank components, all made by a single supplier. It's easy to repair and replace these parts, but not all hardware stores carry them. Plumbing wholesalers do, but they don't often sell to non-plumbers. Plumbers may sell the parts, but they'd rather that you pay for installation as well.

SMART TIP

Which Toilet to Buy? If you need a new toilet, which toilet should you buy: a pressure-assisted model or a gravity-flow unit? Price is one consideration. Pressure-assisted toilets are more expensive than conventional models, upwards of $300. Past experience and the condition of your existing plumbing is another consideration. If your old toilet clogged frequently or you have a system that is more than 50 years old, a pressure-assisted unit is probably your best bet. If you've had few clogs with your old toilet, you'll likely get along fine with a 1.6-gpf gravity-flow toilet, but buy a good, moderately priced one and not a bargain-basement model. For the best performance, look for a trap diameter on the large side: they range from $1\frac{5}{8}$ to 2 inches.

Troubleshooting Gravity-Flow Toilets

Now that you know how traditional gravity-flow toilets are supposed to work, it's time to learn how and why they may not work and what to do when they don't. Keep in mind that poorly maintained toilets may display more than one symptom.

Slow Toilet

Your toilet seems sluggish. It once flushed vigorously, but now the water seems to move slowly through its cycle, often rising high in the bowl before passing through the trap. You also notice large bubbles rising out of the trap during the flush. Sometimes the bowl even seems to double flush.

These are classic symptoms of a partially blocked trap. An obstruction, such as a toy, comb, cotton swab, and the like, has made its way to the top of the trap and lodged in the opening. Paper then begins to accumulate on the obstruction, further closing the opening. In many cases, enough of the trap remains open to keep the toilet working, but in time, partial clogs become complete clogs.

To clear a blockage, start with a toilet plunger, forcing the cup forward and pulling it back with equal pressure. If a plunger doesn't clear the clog, try a closet auger. If the closet auger fails, bail out the bowl with a paper cup or other small container, and place a pocket mirror in the outlet. Shine a flashlight onto the mirror, bouncing light to the top of the trap. The mirror should allow you to see the obstruction. When you know what and where it is, you should be able to pull it into the bowl by using a piece of wire. In rare cases, you may need to remove the toilet and work from the other side.

Slow Toilet Fix

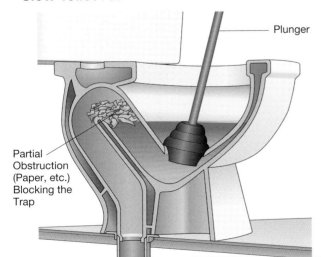

Plunger

Partial Obstruction (Paper, etc.) Blocking the Trap

Cleaning a Bacteria-Clogged Toilet

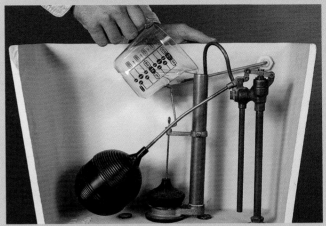

1 To kill bacteria buildup in and under the toilet bowl's rim, pour a bleach solution directly into the overflow tube.

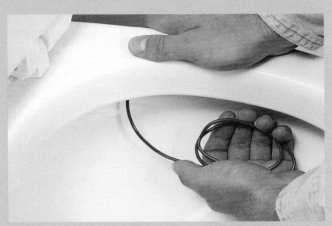

2 Clear bacteria from the rim holes using a short length of insulated electrical wire. Try approaching the hole from several angles.

3 Clear bacteria from the siphon jet (opposite the trap), again using a piece of wire. A dark opening may indicate the presence of bacteria.

Replacing a Flapper

If you hear trickling water, the flapper or tank ball may be worn out. To replace a flapper, shut off the water; unhook the chain; and lift the flapper from its pegs at the base of the flush valve or from around the overflow tube if the flapper has a collar. Before installing the new flapper, clear the valve seat of any old rubber (slime) or mineral deposits. Wipe the seat rim using a paper towel; then sand it lightly using fine sandpaper, steel wool, or an abrasive pad. You may need to use vinegar to dissolve mineral deposits.

The new flapper will likely have two types of flush-valve attachments for a universal fit: side tabs that hook over the valve's side pegs and a rubber collar for use on valves without side pegs. In the latter case, you'd slide the collar over the overflow tube. If side pegs are present at the base of the flush valve, cut the rubber collar from the flapper and throw it away. Then hook the flapper tabs over the pegs. Once you've attached the flapper, reconnect the chain.

1 Clean the flush-valve seat by wiping it with an abrasive material like steel wool or a scouring pad. Feel for imperfections in the seat's surface.

2 Universal flush-valve flappers are made to fit either of two situations you'll encounter. If the flush valve has no side pegs at the bottom of the overflow tube, slide the collar over the tube (photo A). If it has side pegs, cut off the collar (inset), and hook the eyelets over the pegs (photo B).

Replacing a Tank Ball

If you have a tank ball instead of a flapper and need to replace it, drain the tank and remove the tank ball from the lift wire. Thread the lift wire into the new tank ball (right), and check its operation through several flushes. This replacement type has a weighted bottom. It's also a good idea to clean the valve seat using a scouring pad.

Replacing a Flush Valve

1 Loosen the tank bolts with a socket wrench while backholding the slotted bolt head within the tank using a flat-blade screwdriver.

2 Remove the old flush valve's spud-nut washer (inset), and loosen the spud nut using groove-joint pliers. The nut should break free easily.

3 Thread the large spud nut onto the new flush valve at the bottom of the tank, and tighten the nut with pliers until it squeaks.

4 Fit the large rubber spud washer over the spud nut, and coat the washer with a generous layer of pipe joint compound.

5 Install washers on the tank bolts, and coat them with pipe joint compound. Insert the bolts through the tank and bowl.

Retrofit Kits to the Rescue

If you're not up to separating the tank from the bowl to repair a damaged flush valve or if the toilet has its flush valve and overflow cast into the china, then a retrofit valve-seat replacement kit is a good choice. (Eljer and Crane are two manufacturers that may have toilets with these parts cast into the body of the tank.) The kit is an assembly that consists of a stainless-steel or plastic valve seat, an epoxy-putty ring, and a flapper. The super-tough epoxy-putty ring adheres the entire unit onto the old seat. The kit can be used over brass, china, or plastic flush valves.

To install a retrofit valve-seat kit, start by shutting off the water and flushing the toilet to drain the tank. Sponge the remaining water from the tank. Remove the old flapper. If your toilet has a tank ball, remove the ball, the lift wire, and the lift-wire guide. Then sand the old seat to remove mineral deposits and to abrade the sur-face for better adhesion. (You may want to use vinegar if the mineral deposits are stubborn.) Wipe the seat clean, and allow the seat rim to dry.

With the old seat ready, peel one waxed-paper pro-tector from the epoxy ring, and stick the ring to the bot-tom side of the retrofit seat. Peel the remaining waxed paper from the epoxy (photo at bottom left), and press the assembly firmly onto the old valve seat (photo at bot-tom middle). Finally, connect the flapper chain (photo at bottom right), and turn the water back on.

Epoxy kits are not your only valve-seat repair option. A simpler kit consists of a tube of silicone adhesive, which cures under water, and a plastic replacement valve seat. Sand the seat, and then apply a bead of silicone to the seat rim. Press the new seat in place; install a new flapper; and turn the water back on.

1 Peel the protective paper from the epoxy ring.

2 Press the replacement seat over the old seat.

3 Connect the chain with about ½ in. of slack.

Replacing a Fill Valve

If you're having trouble with a toilet's fill valve, it's usually best to replace the entire unit. You'll see several types on the market. The most familiar is probably the traditional ball-cock, in brass or plastic, but you'll also see some that have floats that slide up and down on a vertical riser and some low-profile valves that are activated by head-water pressure.

Codes require fill valves to have built-in backflow protection. Backflow preventers keep tank water from back-siphoning into the water system. Although all codes require them, some manufacturers make both protected and non-protected fill valves. Check the product labeling, and choose a valve that lists built-in backflow prevention as one of its features.

Remove the Old Ballcock. To remove the old fill valve (ballcock), start by shutting off the water and flushing the toilet. Sponge any remaining water from the bottom of the tank. Loosen the coupling nut that binds the supply tube to the ballcock shank. Then loosen the compression nut that binds the bottom of the supply tube to the shutoff valve. Finally, remove the jamb nut from the ballcock shank, and lift the old assembly from the tank.

Install the New Valve. Scrape away any old putty or pipe joint compound from the area around the tank opening. Slide the sealing washer onto the new fill valve's threaded shank, and coat the bottom of the washer with pipe joint compound. Insert the shank through the tank hole, and

Replacing a Fill Valve

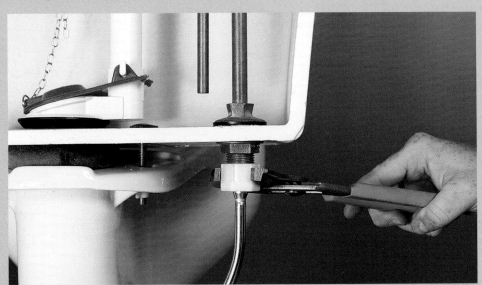

1 Using a pair of large groove-joint pliers, loosen the coupling nut that connects the supply riser to the ballcock shank.

4 While holding the unit steady, carefully tighten the fill valve's jamb nut using pliers until the nut feels snug and begins to squeak.

5 Measure, cut, and install the fill tube. Don't allow it to kink. Connect one end to the fill valve and the other to the overflow tube.

thread the jamb nut onto the shank threads. Before tightening the jamb nut, make sure the fill valve is aligned properly in the tank. If you're installing a traditional-style ballcock with a float ball, make sure the ball doesn't contact the tank wall or the overflow tube. Ideally, the ball should ride at least ½ inch away from the back of the tank. Grip the fill valve to keep it from rotating against the fill tube, and then tighten the jamb nut until the sealing washer flattens out and the nut feels snug.

Next, install the fill tube between the nipple on the fill valve and the flush valve's overflow tube. Use the provided fitting to hold the fill tube on the overflow. You can adjust the float (a ball float if you're installing a ballcock) now by approximating where you want the water level. With a vertical fill valve, pinch the stainless-steel adjustment clip on the float rod, and move the float cup up or down until you reach the desired water level.

Hook Up the Supply Line. The last step is to reconnect the water supply. If the new fill valve's shank extends the same amount from the bottom of the tank as the old one's, you can just reconnect the old water supply tube. If the new shank is more than ⅛ inch longer or shorter than the old one, however, you probably need a new supply tube. The easiest to install is a prefitted tube made of polymer plastic encased in stainless-steel mesh. You just attach the couplings at each end of the tube, and you're done. To avoid damaging the tube, tighten the lower end first.

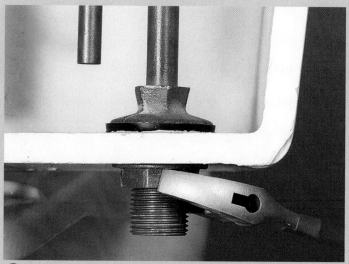

2 Loosen the ballcock jamb nut using an adjustable wrench while gripping the ballcock unit from above.

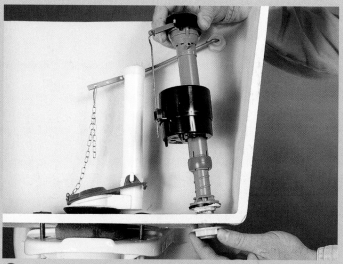

3 Insert the new fill valve through the tank hole, and tighten the jamb nut. Apply pipe joint compound to the washer.

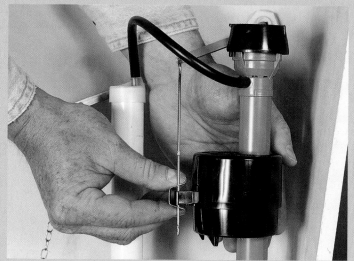

6 Adjust the fill valve's float by compressing and sliding the clip up or down the lift wire. This will control the water level in the tank.

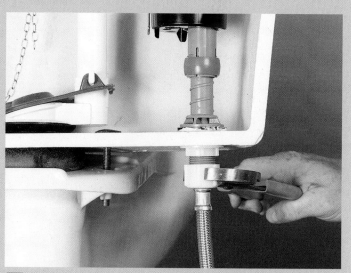

7 Using the pliers again, tighten the supply riser's coupling nut on to the fill valve's exposed shank threads.

Fixing a Running Pressure-Assisted Toilet

Pressure-assisted toilets function differently from gravity-flow toilets. They are based on a different operating principle: use of air pressure. The toilets offer limited repair options, but you can attempt a few remedies.

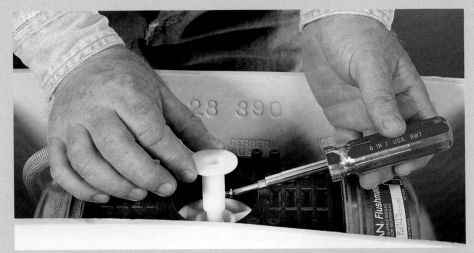

1 Adjust the flush activator setscrew so that the flush button (if you have one) has at least ⅛ in. of clearance before it contacts the activator.

2 If there's no button, adjust the flush lever or activator (or both) as needed so that there is ⅛ in. of clearance between lever and activator.

3 Shut off the water, and using large groove-joint pliers, loosen the jamb nut that holds the water supply group in the tank hole.

4 Twist the supply-group assembly apart to expose the pressure-regulating valve. Install a new valve.

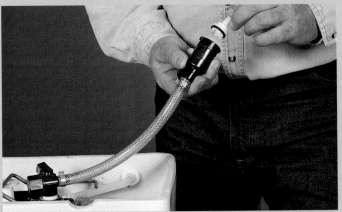

5 Assemble the supply group, and tighten all connections using an adjustable wrench. Backhold nuts using pliers or another wrench.

Cleaning a Fouled Air Inducer

1 With the tank drained, remove the inducer's plastic nut. Place a hand under the inducer to catch the parts.

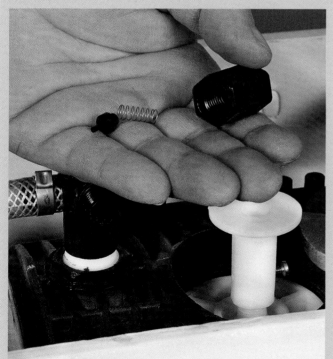

2 Hold the tiny brass or plastic poppit fitting under running water, and roll it between your fingers to clean it.

Replacing a Flush-Valve Cartridge

1 Insert the pointed ends of a large pair of needle-nose pliers into the fins of the cartridge's top nut.

2 Coat the top threads and adjacent O-ring with plumber's grease, and install the cartridge. (Some models do not receive a coating of grease.)

To test for a leaky flush-valve cartridge, remove the water-tank top, pour water around the activator stem, and flush. The appearance of bubbles indicates a leak.

Toilet Flanges

A toilet flange, or closet flange, is a slotted ring, usually connected to a vertical collar. The collar fits through the floor, while the slotted ring, or flange, rests on top of the floor. Toilets are bolted directly to this fitting. In the case of a cast-iron flange, the collar slides over a riser pipe, which extends to floor level. The gap between the pipe and collar is packed with lead and oakum. If the pipe is cast iron and the collar is plastic, the gap is bridged by a rubber gasket. With plastic or copper piping, the flange is cemented or soldered to the riser. In all cases, the flange is anchored to the floor with screws.

When a flange will be installed on concrete, the plumber usually installs a plastic or styrofoam spacer around the waste-pipe riser. The concrete installer then finishes around the spacer, and when the time comes, the plumber removes the spacer and installs the flange. The spacer, in this case, provides fitting room for the flange collar. While this is the most common approach, some jurisdictions allow a simpler method. In these cases, the plumber installs a plastic waste pipe at grade level and tapes it off. The concrete installer then finishes right up to the pipe. When it's time to set the toilet, the plumber cuts out the tape, drills holes in the concrete, and installs anchors for flange mounting screws. The plumber then screws a simple flange ring to the concrete floor. There is no direct connection between the flange and the waste pipe. A concrete-installation wax ring with a seep-proof insert keeps the joint from leaking.

Leaky Flange Gaskets

If you see water on the floor around the toilet, first try to determine whether it is from leaking tank bolts or condensation. If you can't find the source or if more water appears with each use, the water is probably coming from the floor flange. Correct the situation as soon as possible. Water can delaminate plywood, blister underlayment, and rot the subfloor.

Quick Fix. If the toilet was installed within the past few months, then merely tightening the closet bolts on the base of the toilet may reseal the bowl's wax gasket. New wax gaskets almost always compress a little after installation, which can leave the bolts loose. Continued use can then cause the toilet to rock in place, breaking the seal. There's often enough wax to create a new seal—but only if you can draw the toilet and floor flange together.

Start by popping the caps from the closet bolts at the base of the toilet. Pry under them with a screwdriver or putty knife. With the caps removed, use a small wrench to test the tightness of the nuts. If they turn easily, tighten them only until they feel snug, and then watch the base of the toilet carefully over the next few days. If the floor stays dry, you've solved the problem.

Replacing the Gasket. If water reappears or if the bolts were snug in the first place, you'll need to take up the toilet and install a new wax gasket and closet bolts. (See "Taking Up and Resetting a Toilet," page 54.)

Installing Toilet Flanges on a Wood Subfloor

1 This plastic insert flange fits neatly inside a cast-iron riser.

2 Apply PVC cement to the flange and riser, and press in place.

3 Attach the flange to the floor using panhead screws.

Fifty years ago, the gasket material used to set toilets was plumber's putty. The plumber simply rolled out a quantity of putty and pressed it onto the flange. Putty, however, hardens with age, which can lead to leaks. The reason putty worked at all is because toilet bowls back then had four closet bolts instead of the two used today. Two were inverted, through the flange, as they are on modern toilets, but two more bolts located near the front of the flange anchored the bowl to the floor. Four bolts allowed very little flexing.

Wax. Beeswax rings, called bowl wax gaskets, eventually replaced putty as the preferred gasket material for toilets. (You'll also see the rings referred to as wax seals.) These wax rings were able to accommodate the slight flexing that occurs between a toilet and floor, so for generations bowl wax gaskets have been and still are the standard. You can buy gaskets in 3- or 4-inch-diameter sizes by about 1 inch thick. They are inexpensive and durable—a hard combination to beat.

Still, improvements are always in the works. One improvement was to incorporate a plastic, funnel-like insert in the traditional wax gasket. The insert was designed to deliver the water well past the flange surface, thereby eliminating leaks between floor flange and the wax. These special seep-proof gaskets are often used when a toilet is installed on a concrete slab.

Rubber. Next in the progression came flexible-rubber gaskets, which when compressed, block the lateral

migration of water. Rubber gaskets can also reseal themselves once disturbed, and they're reusable. They are sold in several thicknesses to accommodate a variety of flange heights relative to floor height, and you need to buy precisely the right thickness (unlike wax gaskets, which are more forgiving of small height differences). If a rubber gasket is even a little too thick, the toilet won't rest on the floor. If it's too thin, it won't seal.

The benefits of rubber and wax have recently been incorporated into a hybrid gasket, a neoprene rubber ring with a wax coating. (These gaskets are also available with seep-proof inserts.) The advantage is that the rubber will bounce back to reseal itself, while the layer of wax is more forgiving of sizing errors.

Measuring for Rubber. Wax gaskets come in standard thicknesses, and easily conform to slight job-site differences (flooring thickness and the like). In most cases, just knowing the horn length is good enough. To get the right thickness for a rubber flange gasket, you need to lay a straightedge across the base of the toilet and measure the length of the horn. Subtract the thickness of the toilet flange (minus any finish flooring such as tile), and add $\frac{1}{8}$ to $\frac{1}{4}$ inch. The result is the ideal gasket thickness. Buy one as close to that thickness as possible. Measuring is not difficult, but it is bothersome. For that reason, you should use rubber gaskets only when the toilet is likely to be bumped frequently, as it might be when used by a physically handicapped person. A rubber gasket is better able to reseal itself after being disturbed.

Wax and Rubber Flange Gaskets

Neoprene Gasket with Wax Coating

Foam-Rubber Gasket

Wax Gasket with Seep-Proof Insert

Standard Wax Gasket

Resetting a Toilet

Start by shutting off the water. Flush the toilet, holding the handle down to drain as much water as possible from the tank. Use a paper cup or other small container to scoop the water from the bowl, and use a sponge to soak up and discard all of the remaining water in the bowl and tank.

Loosen the coupling nut that joins the water supply tube to the fill valve. Pry the caps from the closet bolts at the base of the bowl, and remove the nuts and washers from these bolts. If the bolts spin in the flange slot, keeping the nuts from threading off, try jamming them to one side so that they bind in the flange slot or against the toilet base. If this doesn't work, use needle-nose pliers to grip the top of the bolts while backing the nuts off. If all else fails, use a miniature hacksaw to cut through the bolts, just under the nuts.

With all connections undone, put down several layers of newspaper to protect the floor from the wax clinging to the outlet. Before moving the toilet to the newspapers, consider how you'll lift and carry it. A toilet is not terribly heavy, and one person can lift it with the right approach. Because the tank will make the toilet back-heavy when it clears the floor, the best place to grip the bowl is just in front of the tank. This deck area will have a lip, making it easy to grip. (Never lift a toilet by its tank.) Straddle the bowl, and with your feet just forward of the tank, tip the toilet up on one side. This will break the wax seal. Still straddling the bowl, carefully raise the toilet several inches and walk (duck-walk) it over to the waiting newspapers. (Rest your elbows on your knees when walking a toilet several feet.) Carefully lay the toilet on its side, and use a putty knife to scrape away any wax clinging to the bottom of the toilet.

Scrape the remaining wax from the surface of the flange, and slide the old closet bolts from their slots. Each slot has a large opening at one end where you can free the bolt head and remove the bolt. If you've cut off the old bolts, buy two bolts, nuts, and metal washers (usually as a kit), as well as a new wax gasket for the bowl. When shopping for a wax gasket, match your piping system's flange size, either 3 or 4 inches.

Set the Toilet. Slide the bolts into their slots, and center them across the outlet opening from each other, typically 12 inches from the wall. Then press the wax gasket onto the flange. Some sources suggest sticking the new gasket to the toilet, but when it's installed on the flange, the gasket keeps the bolts in place. In fact, you should make sure that each bolt is stuck to the wax gasket in an upright position. These bolts guide the toilet onto the flange, so it's important that they remain upright and centered.

To set the toilet, grip it near the hinge deck as before, and walk it over to the flange. Lift it just enough to clear the

Taking Up and Resetting a Toilet

1 Unscrew the compression nut from the toilet shutoff valve. Then loosen the coupling nut at the top of the supply tube.

2 Unscrew the closet-bolt nuts; grip the toilet in front of the seat hinges; lift using your legs; and carry the toilet to many layers of newspaper.

3 Clean old wax from the bottom of the toilet. Install the new closet bolts and wax gasket. Set the toilet over the bolts, and press it into the wax.

waiting closet bolts. Maneuver the toilet until you can see the closet bolts through the holes in the base of the bowl. When the bolts are visible, slowly lower the toilet onto the wax gasket. Check the alignment of the tank: the back of the tank should be parallel with the wall. If it isn't, rotate the toilet left or right until it is straight. Then press down on the rim of the bowl with all your weight. This will compress the wax enough for you to install the nuts on the closet bolts.

Secure the Toilet. If the decorative caps that covered the old closet bolts snapped over plastic retaining washers, install these washers under the metal washers that came with the closet-bolt kit. These plastic keeper-washers are marked "This Side Up." Place the plastic retainers over the bolts first, followed by the metal washers and the nuts. With the bolts ready, draw the nuts down with a 6-inch adjustable or combination wrench, alternating sides every few turns. Using a small wrench allows you to feel the resistance of the nut.

Continue drawing the nuts down until you feel resistance. Don't overtighten, or you'll break the toilet base. When the nuts feel snug, stop, and put all your weight on the bowl again. This will probably loosen the nuts enough to gain another turn with the wrench. Repeat this press-and-wrench sequence until the nuts no longer loosen under your weight. Then, using a miniature hacksaw, cut the bolts just

above the nuts. This may loosen the bolts, so retighten them as needed. Normally, a plumber would snap the decorative caps over the bolts at this point, but because you live in the house, leave them off for a few days. After some use, the nuts will probably loosen slightly. At this point, tighten them again, and then snap the caps in place. If your bolt caps don't have retainer washers, fill them with plumber's putty and press them over the nuts.

Hook Up the Water. You may be able to reuse the water supply tube. Just coat the washer with pipe joint compound, and tighten the nut over the fill-valve shank. If you've damaged the tube or it's old and you just want to replace it, use a new stainless-steel mesh tube. Water supply tubes made of stainless-steel mesh are more convenient to use than other types and are not unattractive if they're visible. Attach and tighten the valve end of the tube first. Use two wrenches, one to tighten the compression nut and one to backhold the shutoff valve. Then attach the tank end of the tube. Turn the coupling nut onto the fill-valve shank until it's finger-tight; then snug it using a pair of groove-joint pliers. Don't overtighten the nut.

Finally, turn the water back on, and test your work. As always, look for leaks at the tank bolts. If the bolts are wet, tighten them just a little. Don't overtighten them, however, and risk cracking the toilet.

4 Tighten the closet-bolt nuts using a small adjustable wrench (for a better feel), and stop when they feel moderately snug.

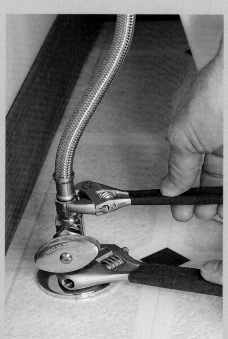

5 While backholding the shutoff valve using one wrench, tighten a new supply tube in place using another.

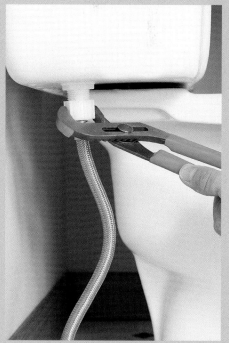

6 Finish by tightening the coupling nut using pliers. Stop when the nut feels snug and begins to squeak.

sinks & faucets

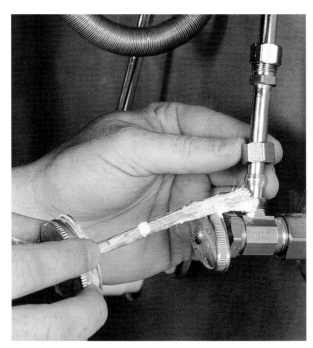

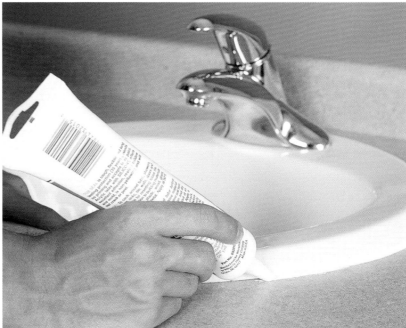

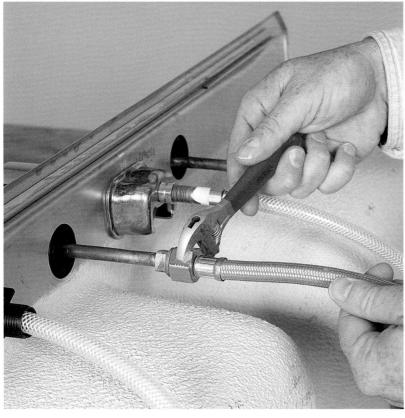

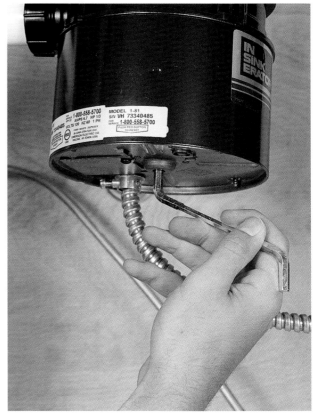

Basic Approaches

There comes a time when those old faucets and sinks just have to go. And given the range of products on home center shelves these days, you're sure to find something you'd like to take home.

Product options range from simple faucet or drain replacement to complete sink and fixture upgrades. In the bathroom, you might also want to add a new vanity cabinet and top, which in many cases are almost a piece of the sink. Or you may be adding a new bathroom, which means the installation of new vanities and sinks.

In the kitchen, replacing the sink and faucet with newer models is a quick way to upgrade the look and functionality of the room. In addition, you might want to add or replace a waste-disposal unit or perhaps an instant hot-water dispenser. These days, you'll find dishwashers (and often waste-disposal units) installed in nearly every new home as original equipment, and instant hot-water dispensers are becoming ever-more-popular kitchen add-ons. Besides covering the removal and installation of these fittings, fixtures, and appliances, this chapter explains how careful maintenance and judicious use can add to the efficiency and longevity of important household products such as and waste-disposal units.

Sink-Connection Basics

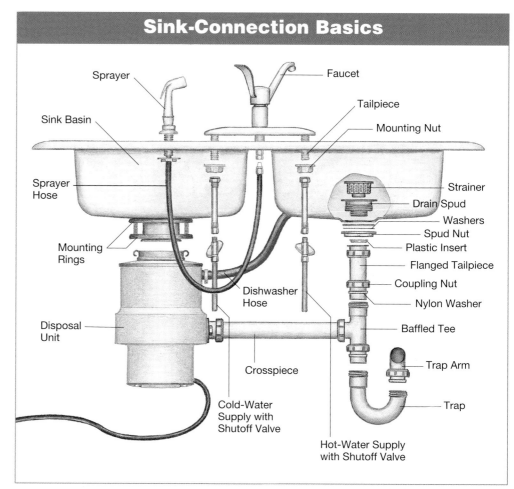

Vanity Sink Anatomy

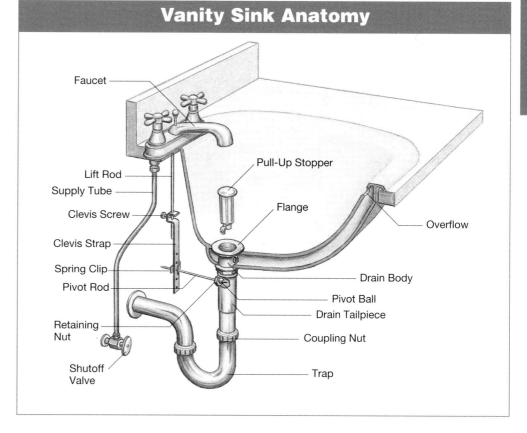

How To Replace a Bathroom Faucet & Drain

Bathroom faucets are sold with and without drain assemblies. Because the lift rod that operates the drain's pop-up plug is installed through the faucet-body cover, it's a good idea to replace both when changing out an old faucet. The procedure described here assumes that your sink is installed in a vanity cabinet.

First, remove the old faucet and drain assembly. Shut off the water, and drain the faucet lines. If you have to shut off the main valve and you have plumbing fixtures on the floor above this bath, open those fixtures as well. Otherwise, water from upstairs will drain onto you as you lie beneath your work.

Removing Old Bathroom Faucets

How you remove the old faucet depends on whether it's a top-mounted or bottom-mounted faucet. Top-mounted faucets are the most common.

Top-Mounted Faucets. A top-mounted faucet is held in place from below by threaded shanks or fastening bolts, which fit through the basin's deck holes. If the faucet is a two-handle model, expect to find jamb nuts tightened onto the shanks from below. In this case, you'll connect the supply tubes to the ends of the shanks. If your faucet has copper tubes instead of brass shanks—usually the case with single-control faucets—the faucet will be held in place by

threaded bolts that protrude through the deck.

When working within the cramped spaces behind a sink, you'll find loosening and tightening nuts a lot easier with a basin wrench. A basin wrench is really just a horizontal wrench on a vertical handle. Lay its spring-loaded jaws to one side, and the wrench loosens, lay it to the other, and it tightens. The extended handle allows you to work high up under a basin or sink deck without having to reach. Loosen the two coupling nuts that secure the supply tubes to the faucet. Then, using a standard adjustable wrench, disconnect the lower ends of the tubes from their compression fittings. Set the supply tubes aside, and use the basin wrench to remove the fastening nuts from the faucet shanks or fastening bolts. Finally, lift the old faucet from its deck holes.

Bottom-Mounted Faucets. If the old faucet is a bottom-mounted model, with the body of the faucet installed below the sink deck, the initial approach is from above. Leave the supply tubes in place until after you've completed your work on top. Start by prying the index caps from the faucet handles. Remove the handle screws, and lift the handles from their stems. This will give you access to the flanges (or escutcheons) threaded onto the stem columns. Thread these flanges off; disconnect the supply tubes; and drop the faucet from its deck. Some bottom-mounted faucets consist of three isolated components, including two stems and a spout. These components are joined with tubing and are easy to disassemble from below.

Removing Faucets

To remove a **top-mounted faucet**, use a basin wrench to unscrew the jamb nuts from the faucet shanks.

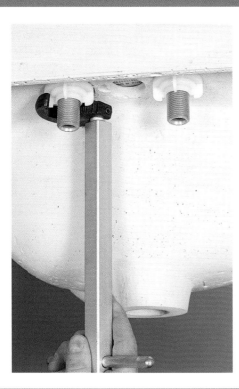

To remove a **bottom-mounted faucet**, undo the connecting tubing and remove the jamb nuts.

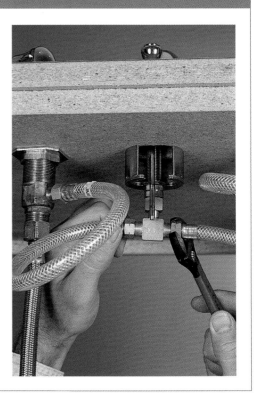

Removing the Drain

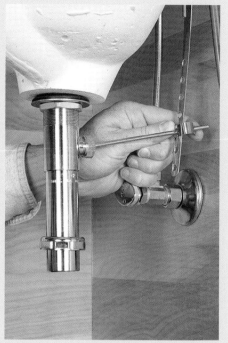

1 To remove a sink-basin drain, loosen the two P-trap nuts and remove the trap. Keep a bucket under the trap to catch wastewater.

2 To remove the P-trap arm, disconnect the friction nut at the wall and pull the arm straight out from the drainpipe.

3 To disconnect the sink drain's pop-up linkage, squeeze the tension clip and slide the clevis from the lever.

4 Use groove-joint pliers to loosen the nut that holds the sink drain in place. Backhold the drain using a second pair of pliers if it spins.

5 Unscrew the basin flange from the sink drain (working from above), and pull the drain out of the basin from below.

SMART TIP

Drain Variations. The drain assembly described in "Removing the Drain," is the most common type, but it's not the only one available. Some drain assemblies don't have a threaded flange at the top. In this case, the top of the extension tube is flared to form a flange, which means that you'll need to back the fastening nut completely from the extension. The problem is the lever housing will get in the way. To remove this type of drain, you'll first need to unscrew the lever housing from the extension. When you have the housing and the fastening nut removed, you'll be able to lift the extension out from above.

Installing a New Bathroom Faucet

Installing a new faucet is not particularly difficult. If the faucet comes with a plastic or rubber base-plate gasket, put the gasket on it before setting it in place. If the new faucet has threaded brass shanks, insert the shanks through the deck holes; center the faucet; and align the back of the base plate with the wall. Then thread a jamb nut onto each shank from below, and tighten the nuts with a basin wrench keeping the faucet straight and centered.

If the faucet does not have threaded brass shanks (as most single-control faucets do not), expect to find two bolts alongside two copper tubes. When you have inserted the tubes and bolts through the deck and positioned the faucet, install an extended locking washer and a nut on each bolt, and tighten it all down. (To connect the water supply tubes, see "Connecting the Water," page 66.)

Installing the New Drain

To install the drain assembly, first find the drain flange ring. Stick the putty to the underside of the flange, and set the flange aside for the moment.

The drain tube should come with its hex nut, brass washer, and rubber gasket already in place. Apply a thin coating of pipe joint compound to the rubber gasket. Push the drain up through the bottom of the sink basin using one hand, and working from above, thread the flange onto the drain.

With the two halves joined, orient the opening for the pop-up lever to the back of the sink, and tighten the hex nut. Stop when the nut feels snug and the rubber washer is compressed against the basin outlet. Return topside, and trim the excess putty from around the flange using a knife. Then drop the lift rod through the opening in the top of the faucet. Next, insert the pop-up plug into the drain so that its offset slot faces the back of the basin. It should rest on top of the lever, slightly above the closed position. (If you want a pop-up that is removable, turn the offset toward the front of the basin.)

To engage the pop-up plug using the lift lever, loosen the nut that secures the lever in the drain tube. Withdraw the lever slightly, until you hear the pop-up plug drop, and then push the lever forward, into the plug's slot. Screw the lever's nut back into place, but stop when you begin to feel resistance. Connect the lever to the second or third clevis hole from the bottom, and squeeze the clip onto the lever.

1 With the old faucet removed, set the base-plate gasket in place and insert the faucet's water lines through the deck holes.

4 If it's not already in place, slide the cone-shaped gasket onto the drain and coat it with pipe joint compound.

7 Lower the faucet's drain-plug lift rod through the hole in the top of the faucet until it bottoms out.

Faucet and Drain

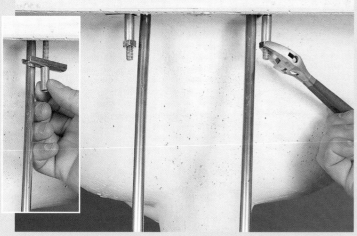

2 Install the extended washers and the spacers (inset), and thread the nuts onto the faucet's fastening bolts.

3 With the faucet installed, press a roll of plumber's putty around the underside of the drain flange.

5 Insert the drain through the basin's drain opening from below, and thread the flange ring onto it from above.

6 Tighten the hex-shaped jamb nut using groove-joint pliers until it feels snug; then trim away the excess putty from above.

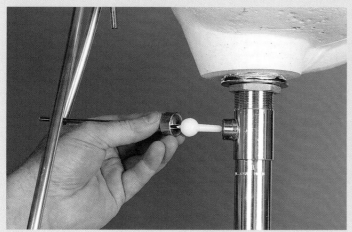

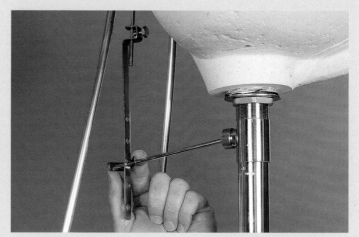

8 Insert the pop-up assembly.

9 Connect the clevis through one of the lower holes (with the lever pointing down), and install the clip.

Installing a Metal-Rim Sink

1 Drill ¼-in.-or-larger holes in one or more corners of the marked cutout, and follow the pencil mark using a saber saw to cut the hole for the sink.

2 Use a screwdriver to bend the tabs inward on the sink rim. With a cast-iron sink, install supporting corner brackets as well.

3 Use a sink-clip wrench (or a long nut driver or screwdriver) to drive the clip bolts against the underside of the counter.

SMART TIP

Plumber's putty has long been used to seal rim-style sinks. However, plumber's putty can turn dark—or even black—and grows brittle with age, cracking and chipping. Fortunately, there are better products for the job. A good choice for today's sink installation is a bead of tub-and-tile caulk. The best kind to use is PVA (polyvinyl acetate) caulk, acrylic latex caulk, or silicon caulk. Any of those types will work fine and remain fairly flexible for a long time, but be sure you buy tub-and-tile caulk that is mildew resistant. Otherwise, it may turn black like plumber's putty. Once you've installed the sink, clean up any caulk that squeezes out from around the sink.

Installing a Self-Rimming Cast-Iron Sink

Cast iron is heavy and expensive, so call a friend if you think you need help. With one of you on each side, lift the sink over the counter and into the sink opening. When it's set, carefully move it around until you have it centered and straight, relative to the backsplash. Don't be too concerned if the sink rocks in place. Some sinks become a little warped in the firing process. A warp of ¼ inch is acceptable, because when you've balanced and shimmed the sink corner to corner, you'll be able to fill the two ⅛-inch gaps using caulk. A warp greater than ¼ inch is too much. Insist on a replacement. In any case, wait until the sink is hooked up and tested before doing any caulking.

Attaching Drain Fittings to the New Sink

You will need to install a basket-strainer drain in each of the sink's drain outlets, unless you plan on putting in a waste-disposal unit. (See "Installing a Waste-Disposal Unit," page 70.) Drain kits come with a removable basket strainer and a drain body, large spud nut, paper washer, rubber washer, and coupling nut. You will also need plumber's putty to seal the flange on the drain body.

Begin by setting the new sink on a worktable or on the kitchen floor near the sink cabinet. To keep from damaging the table or floor, place the sink on a piece of cardboard. Separate all drain components. Then roll a handful of putty between your hands until you form a rope roughly ½ inch thick and 10 inches long, and stick the putty to the underside of the drain flange.

Insert the drain through the sink opening, and press it into place. Working from the underside, slide the rubber washer onto the drain spud, followed by the paper washer and the large spud nut. Using a spud wrench or large groove-joint pliers, tighten the nut until much of the putty is squeezed from the flange inside the sink. Trim away the excess putty using a knife, and tighten some more. Trim the excess putty again, and continue to tighten. When the nut feels tight or the drain begins to spin, stop. For a double sink, install the remaining drain in similar fashion.

Attaching Drain Fittings to the New Sink

1 Form plumber's putty into a ½-in. roll several inches long, and press it against the underside of the drain flange.

2 Insert the drain through the sink opening, and install the rubber gasket, paper gasket, and spud nut in that order.

3 Use a spud wrench or large pliers to tighten the spud nut. Trim any excess putty from around the flange in the sink, and tighten the nut again.

SMART TIP

When removing an existing drain, you sometimes will not be able to budge the spud nut using a standard spud wrench. If that happens, cut the nut in two using a hacksaw.

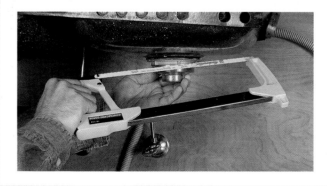

Attaching a Kitchen Faucet

Faucets from different manufacturers differ slightly in the way you mount them, but the basic connections remain the same.

Place the faucet's base plate over the sink's deck holes, and insert the mounting shanks on each side. From underneath, slide a large washer onto each fastening shank, followed by a jamb nut. Turn the nuts until they're finger-tight. Make sure the faucet's base plate is parallel with the back edge of the sink.

If the faucet is a single-handle type with central copper inlet tubes, straighten the tubes; position the decorative deck plate over the base plate; and insert the tubes through the center deck hole. Slide the mounting hardware (either a nut or a screw plate) onto the faucet shaft, and fasten the faucet in place. If the faucet has a pullout spout, connect the spout hose now. Attach the supplied adapter to the faucet nipple. Pull back the spring housing to reveal the male threads of the hose inlet end, and screw the hose into the adapter. Attach the outlet end of the hose to the faucet at the top of the spout housing to complete the connection.

Sinks come with either three or four deck holes. The fourth hole is for accessories like a separate hose sprayer, an instant hot-water dispenser, a soap dispenser, and the like. When codes require a backflow preventer in the dishwasher discharge hose, the fourth deck hole can also hold the backflow preventer. If you can't think of an add-on you'd care to own, plug the opening with a chrome or brass-plated sink-hole cover.

Installing a Kitchen Faucet

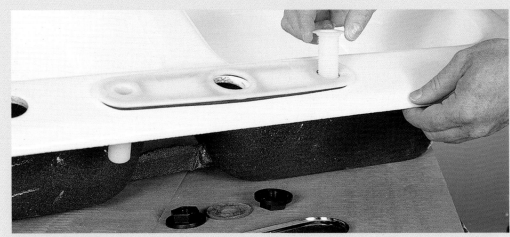

1 Center-column faucets work on sinks with one or three holes. For a multi-hole sink, install a base plate.

4 Slide the mounting hardware onto the column and tighten it. The unit shown has a plastic spacer, steel washer, and brass nut.

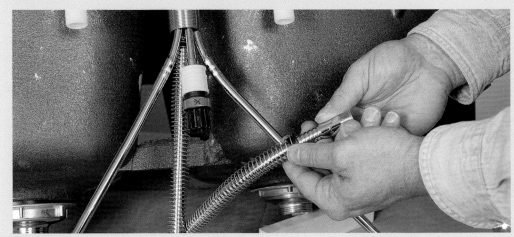

7 Pull back the spiral tension spring at the bottom end of the spray hose to expose the male attachment threads.

2 Fasten the plastic base-plate support/gasket from below using plastic jamb nuts. Make them finger-tight.

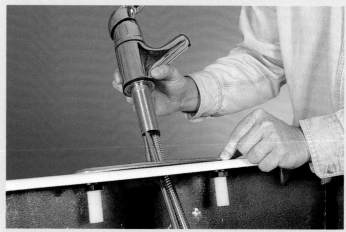

3 Snap the decorative base plate in place over the plastic support, and insert the faucet's column through the center hole in the sink deck.

5 Use a screwdriver to drive the setscrews against the large washer. Stop when the screws feel snug.

6 Install the supply adapter on the faucet nipple. Most faucets use a slip fitting with an O-ring seal, as shown.

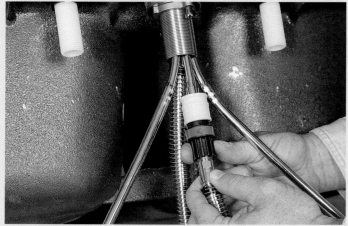

8 Tighten the male threads into the bottom of the faucet's supply adapter. Stop when it feels snug. Don't overtighten it.

9 From above, thread the outlet end of the hose into the spray head. Pull the hose out several times to test it for ease of use.

Connecting the Trap

With two sink basins (each with a strainer-drain), you'll need a plastic sink waste kit and a plastic P-trap to complete the waste hookup. Depending on the rough-in position of the permanent piping, you may also need a tailpiece extension, one that has a female hub and compression fitting at one end. The new sink waste kit will consist of two flanged tailpieces, a baffled T-fitting, a 90-degree extension tube, and assorted nuts and washers. Two of the washers will be insert washers with an L-shaped profile. Insert one of these into the top of each flanged tailpiece. Then slide metal coupling nuts onto the tailpieces, and thread the nuts onto the drain spuds. Next, install the baffled T-fitting on the tailpiece nearest the permanent drain piping.

Mark the 90-degree extension tube for length. Cut the tube with a hacksaw, making sure that you allow for the depth of the T's hub, and attach it to the remaining drain on the 90-degree end and to the T-fitting on the other. Next, hold the assembled P-trap in place. If the trap will fit between the T-fitting and the drain outlet, hook it up directly. If you see a gap between the top of the trap hub and the bottom of the baffled T-fitting, you'll need to lengthen the drain using a fitted tailpiece extension. These extensions come in various lengths and can be cut to fit. If the T-fitting is too long, mark and cut it.

With all the piping ready, connect the trap to the permanent waste pipe in the floor or wall. In a new installation, where a 1½ inch PVC pipe exists in the wall, you'll need to fit this pipe using a ground-joint trap adapter. If you've purchased a plastic P-trap, the adapter will be included. Glue the adapter to the pipe, then connect the trap to the adapter using a compression washer and nut.

Existing Drainpipes. If you're connecting the new trap to an existing drain fitting, expect one of two trap-to-drain arrangements. If the drain line was installed within the past 30 years, you may luck out and get a plastic ground-joint trap adapter. Slightly older homes may have copper or brass adapters. In all three cases, standard compression washers and nuts will make the transition.

But if the permanent piping is made of galvanized steel, expect a friction fit. In this case, substitute a flat rubber washer for the beveled nylon washer included with the trap.

Connecting the Trap

1 Press the nylon insert washer into the flanged tailpiece.

4 Hold the horizontal extension tube (from the other sink, if any) up to the baffled waste T-fitting, and mark the tube to length.

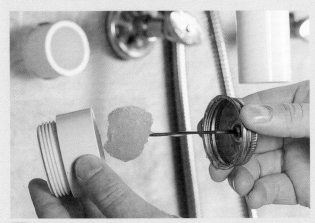

7 Apply PVC primer and cement to the outside of the drainpipe and the inside of the ground-joint adapter, and cement them together.

Connecting the Water

Hold the water supply tube between the faucet stub and the shut-off port, and mark it for length. Account for the depth of the fitting hub. Connect the tube, and install the compression nut and ferrule. Coat the threads and ferrule using pipe joint compound. Tighten the compression nuts at both ends of the supply tube. Backhold the upper fitting.

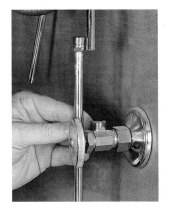

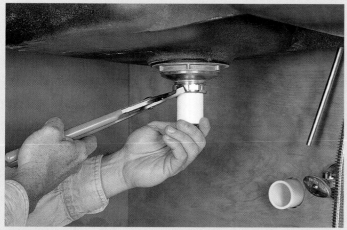

2 Tighten the tailpiece onto the drain spud (on each sink if more than one).

3 Slide a compression nut and beveled, nylon washer onto the tailpiece, and install the baffled T-fitting (for more than one sink).

5 Install a compression nut and washer onto the horizontal extension tube, and tighten the tube in the T-fitting.

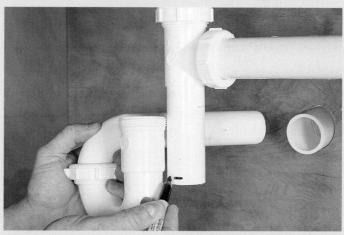

6 In similar fashion to Step 3, hold the trap in place and mark the T-fitting to length. Cut the T-fitting using a hacksaw.

A

B

8 How you make the trap-to-drainpipe connection depends on the piping material at hand. A plastic ground-joint adapter (A) is best with plastic pipe, and a flat, rubber washer and metal nut (B) are best when the drain is made of galvanized steel. A banded coupling is another option, but it costs much more.

Removing a Waste-Disposal Unit

Unlike drain fittings, waste-disposal units don't become hopelessly stuck to sinks. The reason has to do with the mounting mechanisms, which range from simple hose-clamp fasteners to threaded-plastic collars to triple-layer bolt-on assemblies. The triple-layer mechanism described here is the most common—and the most complicated.

To remove an old waste-disposal unit, start by shutting off the electrical power to the unit, either within the sink cabinet or at the main service panel. If your disposal unit also drains a dishwasher, loosen the hose clamp that secures the dishwasher discharge hose and pull the adapter from the waste-disposal-unit nipple. Next, loosen the horizontal waste tube's slip nut at the waste T-fitting, and undo the bolt or compression nut that secures the tube to the side of the disposal unit. Remove this tube.

Disengage the Unit. To release the waste-disposal unit, look for three rolled-edge slots on the mounting ring. The ring is mounted at the top of the unit and has three such slots. Insert a screwdriver into one of the slots, and rotate the ring counterclockwise. If it won't budge, tap it using a hammer.

Removing a Waste-Disposal Unit

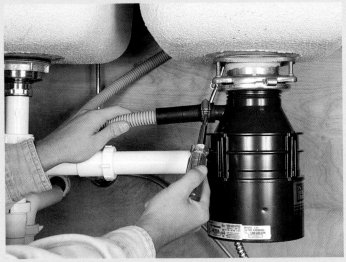

1 Unscrew the hose clamp on the dishwasher discharge hose. Pull the hose from the disposal unit's inlet nipple.

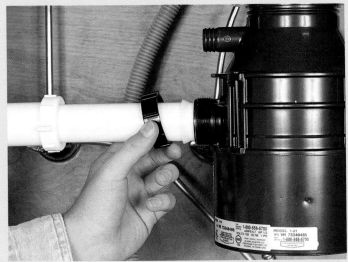

2 Remove the waste connection at the side of the disposal unit. Some are bolted in, and some have compression nuts.

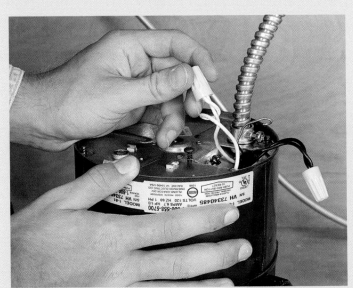

5 With the power shut off at the main panel, reach into the box and pull out the wires. Remove the twist connectors.

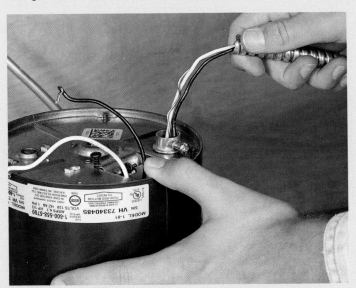

6 Disconnect the ground wire, and loosen the box connector. Pull the conduit and wires from the connector.

As soon as the unit breaks free, support its bottom using one hand and rotate the nut about 2 inches until the unit falls away. This will leave only the bolted drain fitting in place.

With the disposal unit out, loosen the screw that holds the cover plate to the unit's electrical box. Pull the wires from the box, and undo the twist connectors and grounding screw. Then remove the fastening nut from the threaded box connector. This nut is located just inside the box, and you can turn it using your fingers as soon as you knock it loose using the screwdriver. With the nut removed, pull the connector and wires from the unit.

Remove the Drain Fitting. To undo the drain assembly, use a slotted screwdriver to loosen all three bolts separating the layers of the drain. With the bolts unscrewed about ½ inch, push the mounting flange up to reveal the locking ring. Pry this ring from its groove, and all the under-sink components will fall away. Lift the drain from the sink, and scrape away any old putty you find clinging to the basin under the flange. Note: If you're not up to wiring a first-time disposal unit, pull the cable and install the boxes, then hire an electrician to install the breaker and switch.

3 Insert a screwdriver into one of the tabs of the retaining ring as shown, and rotate the ring counterclockwise.

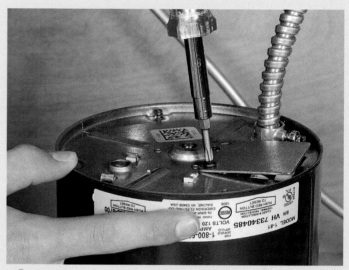

4 Once you have disconnected the disposal unit, lower it and turn it over. Use a screwdriver to remove the electrical box cover.

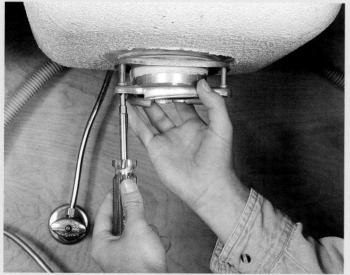

7 To remove the waste-disposal-unit drain fitting from under the sink, loosen the three bolts in the retaining ring.

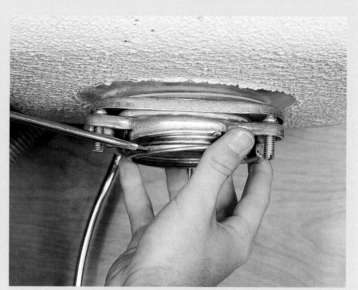

8 With the pressure removed, slide the retaining ring up and use a screwdriver to pry off the snap ring to release the components.

Installing a Waste-Disposal Unit

In a simple one-for-one swap, just install the new waste-disposal unit in reverse order of removal of the old one, using existing wiring and waste fittings. If you're installing your first unit, start with the drain assembly.

Install the Drain Assembly. As with conventional kitchen sink drains, the drain that goes from a sink to a waste-disposal unit needs to be sealed with plumber's putty. Roll fresh room-temperature putty between your hands until you have a rope of it about 10 inches long and ½ inch thick. Press the putty around the underside to the drain flange, and press the flange onto the bottom of the sink at the outlet.

The drain assembly that attaches underneath the sink consists of a gasket, a sealing flange, a bolted flange (with a tapered edge to accept the mounting ring), and a split retaining ring. Turn the flange bolts counterclockwise until they're backed out of the bolted flange most of the way. Next, slide the gasket and the sealing flange onto the drain spud so that the sealing flange's smooth surface faces the sink. Then slide the bolted flange up against the sealing flange, with its slotted-taper facing down. While holding both flanges against the bottom of the sink, slip the retaining ring over the drain spud until it seats in its groove.

With the retaining ring in place, let the flanges down and rotate them until the bolts seat against the sealing flange. Tighten all three bolts, a little at a time, until you've drawn the components together and squeezed most of the putty from the in-sink flange.

With the drain assembly in place, lift the waste-disposal unit up to the drain and engage its mounting ring. Rotate the ring clockwise until you feel stiff resistance. Then insert a screwdriver into one of the rolled-edge slots, and tighten the ring until it stops.

Connect the Waste Kit. Next, you must connect the waste kit. All waste-disposal units come with a 90-degree waste L-fitting. When installing the unit in a single-compartment sink, use the L-fitting to join the P-trap.

With a double sink, however, you don't need the L-fitting. Instead, buy a disposal-unit waste kit, which comes with a straight flanged tailpiece extension instead of the 90-degree waste L-fitting. The kit's assembly procedure is similar to that for installing a conventional sink waste kit. (See "Connecting the Trap," page 66.) The only difference is in how the flanged tailpiece joins the waste-disposal unit. All the parts you'll need, including a flange, a rubber gasket, and one or two bolts, come with the new unit. To make the connection, once you've assembled the rest of the kit, slide the compression washer and slip nut onto the tailpiece. Next, fit the gasket into the waste-disposal unit's outlet, slide the flange onto the tailpiece, and bolt the flange into the unit. Now slide the compression washer and slip nut toward the flange, and tighten the nut. The other end of the tailpiece joins the branch of the kit's waste T-fitting. Finally, remove the dishwasher knockout plug and attach the dishwasher drain hose if you have one. Tighten the hose clamp that's supplied with the unit to complete the connection.

1 Roll plumber's putty in your hands to make a 10-in. length with a diameter of about ½ in. Press it under the drain flange (inset). Slide the mounting assembly (gasket, sealing flange, mounting flange, and split ring) onto the drain spud.

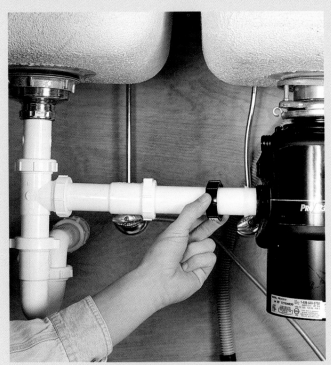

4 Install the horizontal tailpiece extension between the existing second-sink T-fitting and the disposal unit.

Waste-Disposal Unit

2 Install the split ring at the bottom, and turn the flange bolts clockwise using a screwdriver, each in turn a little at a time, until they're snug.

3 Lift the disposal unit to the drain fitting, and engage the mounting ring. Rotate the ring clockwise to secure the unit.

5 If you want to hook up a dishwasher, drive the plug from the disposal unit's dishwasher nipple and connect the discharge hose.

6 Hold a cut-in retrofit electrical box against the wall above the unit, and trace around it. Stay at least 1 in. away from studs.

continued on page 72

continued from page 71

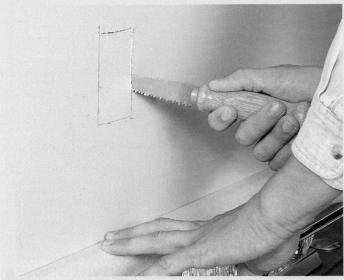

7 Use a utility saw to cut out the opening for the electrical switch box. Work carefully, and try for a tight fit.

8 Pull the cables into the cut-in box, and press the box into the wall. Engage the attachment tabs by tightening the screws.

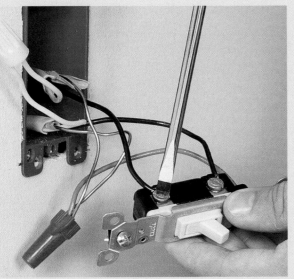

9 Wire the switch using black wires and a grounding pigtail; join the white wires and the grounding wires in separate connectors.

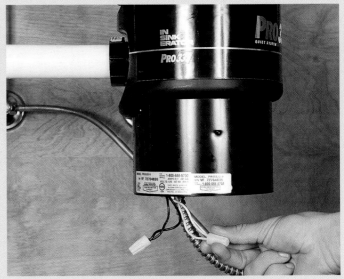

10 Use flex conduit between the wall and disposal unit, and join like-colored wires using twist connectors.

Install the Wiring. Local building codes vary, but don't expect to be able to pull electricity from an existing kitchen circuit to power your new waste-disposal unit. Most kitchen circuits are stretched to the limit already, and circuits with ground-fault circuit-interrupter (GFCI) protection won't be able to handle the startup overcurrent generated by these units. While a disposal unit and instant hot-water dispenser may be able to share a circuit, a disposal unit and dishwasher may not. You should bring a new circuit into the kitchen for a new waste-disposal unit.

Shut off the power at the main electrical service panel, and install a new 15-amp circuit breaker. (If you're not com-fortable installing a circuit breaker, then run the cable between the panel and the waste-disposal unit, make the connection at the unit, and hire a licensed electrician to install the breaker. The job won't cost much this way, and you won't be exposing yourself to 100 amps or more of electricity. Leave at least 4 feet of cable hanging near the panel.) Extend 14/2g cable between the panel and the cabinet wall. Each house will present its own barriers, but look for a basement or attic route of delivery. When you reach the kitchen wall behind the cabinets, drill into the wall, either through its sole plate or top plates. Choose a stud space behind the sink cabinet.

Installing an Instant Hot-Water Dispenser

Instant-hot-water dispensers are custom made for busy lives. At 190 degrees F, the water that these pint-sized appliances serve up is most likely at least 40 to 50 degrees hotter than that delivered by your water heater. (Water heaters are dangerous when used above 140 degrees F.) Water at a temperature of 190 degrees F is just right for blanching vegetables, making instant soups, and brewing real coffee, one cup at a time. Most units deliver 40 to 60 cups of hot water a day. The operating costs are about the same as a 40-watt lightbulb. Dispensers range in price from $90 to $250. The more expensive ones are better insulated and produce more hot water.

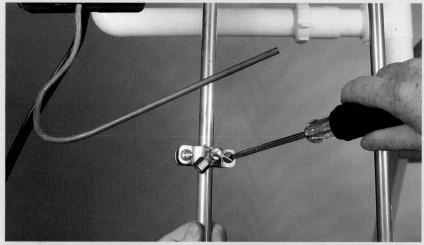

1 Make the water connection using the supplied saddle valve. All you have to do is clamp the valve onto the cold-water line.

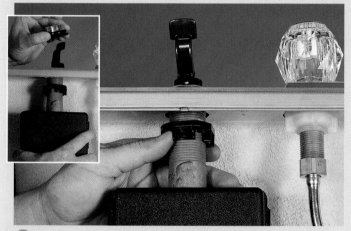

2 Feed the unit through the sink hole, and install the mounting nut from above (inset). Tighten the jamb nut below.

3 Install the spout in the sink-deck fitting, and tighten the faucet's setscrew to secure it. The spout seals using an O-ring.

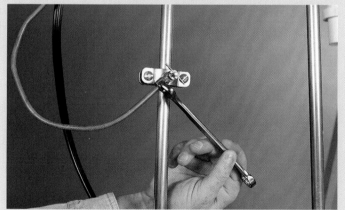

4 Connect the ¼-in. heater water line to the saddle valve using the supplied compression nut and ferrule. Use an open-end wrench as shown.

5 If the heating unit delivers water above or below 190 deg. F, adjust the temperature setting using a flat-blade screwdriver.

faucet repairs

Faucet Overview

Faucet repair is an ideal do-it-yourself project. It's light work, and the parts are affordable—often less than $5 for a complete repair. With compression faucets, the material costs can run closer to 5¢ if you just have to replace a washer. (Hire a professional plumber to repair a faucet, and you will find that labor accounts for most of the bill.) But the longer you wait to fix a faucet, the more expensive a repair will become. A steady drip will eventually destroy important parts in the unit, requiring complete replacement (at a much higher cost than a repair) and wasting hundreds of gallons of water in the process.

Old-fashioned single-inlet faucets could turn a supply of water on and off, but they provided only cold or hot water. To get warm water, you had to mix the hot and cold water in a basin. Dual-inlet faucets, now universally standard, can mix hot and cold water before sending it through the spout. You'll find dual-inlet faucets with four kinds of water-control mechanisms.

- Compression valve
- Cartridge
- Ball valve
- Ceramic disk valve (also usually in a cartridge)

Leakproof Water Control. To make a positive seal against continuous water pressure, one of two things is required: 1) some form of resilient gasket material to fill the gaps between sealing surfaces or 2) companion sealing surfaces that are rock hard and precisely machined for a tight, leakproof fit. Compression, ball-type, and many cartridge faucets use metal or nylon moving parts with neoprene-rubber washers, seals, or O-rings. Other cartridge designs use ceramic disks, which have an extremely hard, smooth surface. Many top-of-the-line faucets use ceramic-disk technology for water control.

There are hundreds of faucet makes and models in use today, each with its proprietary twist. In fact, when working on some older models you might wonder why anyone would clutter such a simple device with so many extra gaskets, spacers, and sleeves. If you come across one of these faucets, don't be overwhelmed. Just replace the extra parts in reverse order of removal, and concentrate on the basics. Discussion of the four basic faucet designs follows. In some cases, you may be able to identify your faucet type by looking at the faucet or identifying its brand. In others, you'll have to take the faucet apart.

Washer-Equipped Compression Faucets

The most familiar faucet may be the washer-equipped compression-type faucet, sold under many brand names. Compression faucets control water by means of threaded, washer-fitted stems that move up and down over brass seats. Every compression faucet consists of a handle, a packing nut and/or bonnet nut, a threaded stem with washer, a washer screw, and a brass seat. The washer fits into the seat to shut off the water.

In two-handle dual-inlet faucets, each inlet port has its own stem. (The compression design doesn't allow for single-handle dual-inlet faucets.) Single-stem compression faucets, including hose bibcocks, sillcocks, boiler drains, and old-fashioned single-inlet faucets, are not mixing valves.

Washerless Faucets

When cartridge faucets first appeared in the late 1950s, they were touted as "washerless" at a time when virtually everyone was familiar with leaky washer faucets. Since then, other washerless designs have been developed, including ball-type and ceramic-disk faucets.

Virtually all washerless faucets operate according to the same design prin-

Cartridge Faucet. With a cartridge faucet, repair usually consists of merely replacing the cartridge.

Compression Faucet. Compression faucets are fitted with a replaceable stem washer for low-cost repair.

ciple: inlet ports are moved into or out of alignment with companion ports in the faucet body. When the openings are aligned, water flows from pipes to spout. When rotated out of alignment, the flow is sliced off. The degree and angle of rotation dictates the volume of the flow and the temperature of the mix. These faucets tend to work trouble-free longer than compression faucets for one very good reason: you can't overtighten a cartridge faucet. While those who grew up with leaky compression faucets instinctively give faucet handles an extra twist, which hastens the destruction of the washer and results in a dripping faucet, washerless faucets can only be tipped or lifted (single-handle models) or rotated one-quarter turn (dual-handle models).

Cartridge. A cartridge faucet may have two handles, like compression faucets, or a single handle. If your faucet is an Aqualine, Moen, Price Pfister, or Valley brand single-handle model, it is probably a cartridge type. If it is a dual-handle model, you'll have to take it apart to tell what kind it is. For repairs, see pages 82 to 84.

Ball-Type. Ball-valve faucets are always single-handle units. The ball contains inlet ports that align with faucet-body ports to allow water flow. Movement of the ports alters the flow rate and hot-cold mixture. Delta and Peerless are the major ball-type faucet brands. For repairs, see pages 80 to 81.

Ceramic Disk. Another single-handle or two-handle design, ceramic-disk faucets contain a cylinder that houses two mating ceramic disks, one with inlet and outlet ports and one without. The disks slide into and out of alignment with each other to control water flow and temperature. If you have an American Standard or Reliant unit, it is likely a ceramic-disk faucet. For repairs, see page 85.

Repairing Compression Faucets

Compression faucets have three basic problem areas, each with its own symptom.

■ If the faucet drips from the end of the spout, you'll have to replace the seat washers and frequently the seats themselves. (See opposite.)

Compression Faucet Anatomy

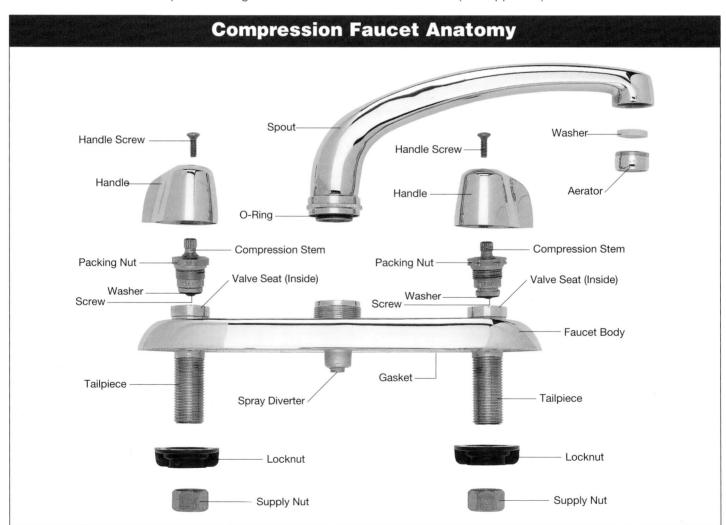

Handle Screw

Handle

O-Ring

Packing Nut

Washer

Screw

Compression Stem

Valve Seat (Inside)

Tailpiece

Spray Diverter

Locknut

Supply Nut

Spout

Handle Screw

Handle

Washer

Aerator

Compression Stem

Packing Nut

Valve Seat (Inside)

Washer

Screw

Faucet Body

Gasket

Tailpiece

Locknut

Supply Nut

■ If the faucet leaks around its handles when the water is turned on but not when the water is shut off, the stem packing is worn, and you should replace it by turning off the water, removing the handle and bonnet nut (see below), and replacing the old packing washer.

Replacing a Seat Washer To Fix a Leak

Compression faucets and valves need repair as soon as you notice them dripping or when their neoprene-rubber washers become old and brittle.

Handles First. To service the faucet, remove the handles after you turn off the water supply at the shutoff valves. Some older faucet models have exposed handle screws. If you don't see handle screws, either in the tops of the handles or on the sides of the handle collars, they are prob-ably hidden under decorative index caps. Index caps are usually marked "H" and "C." To gain access to the handle screws, pry under the index caps with a sharp knife, and set them aside. To keep from reversing the hot- and cold-side stems, work on only one side at a time.

Remove the screw, and lift the handle from the first stem. If the handle won't budge, pry under it with a screwdriver. If it still won't budge, use a handle puller as shown in step 3 below.

With the handle removed, look for the hex-head bonnet nut that locks the stem into the faucet. If you see two nuts, the smaller top nut will most likely be the packing nut and the nut threaded into or over the body will be the bonnet nut. Loosen the bonnet nut. If it binds before you can remove the stem, rotate the stem up or down. This should free the nut, allowing you to easily lift the stem from the faucet body.

Replacing a Seat Washer

1 After shutting off the water supply at the shutoff valve, pry the index cap from the handle with a sharp tool like a utility knife.

2 Use a screwdriver to remove the handle screw from the handle. The screw is most likely to be a Phillips-head type.

3 If you can't lift off the handle, it's best to use a handle puller. Drive the stem of the puller into the screw hole.

4 Use an adjustable wrench to loosen the bonnet nut. If the nut binds, turn the stem counterclockwise as far as it will go and try again.

continued on page 78

6 Faucet Repairs

continued from page 77

5 Lift the stem to expose the seat washer and screw.

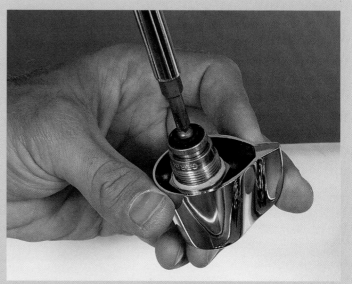

6 Reattach the handle to make working on the stem easier, and remove the washer screw.

7 Choose the correct size and shape replacement washer for your faucet (by examining the valve seat), and press it into the stem's retainer.

8 Tighten the washer screw in place, and coat the washer and stem threads with heat-proof faucet grease before reinstalling the stem.

Expect to find a worn or broken rubber seat washer attached to the stem. Put the handle back on the stem to make it easier to work on. To remove the washer, back the screw off the end of the stem. Carefully pry the washer from the stem using a sharp knife.

Before replacing the seat washer, decide whether you should use a flat or beveled one. (The person before you may have installed the wrong type of washer, so don't assume the one you took out is what your faucet needs.) Examine the brass seat. (This is also a good time to check the seat for damage.) If the faucet's seat has a raised rim, approximately 1/16 inch tall, use a flat washer. If the

seat is concave, without a pronounced rim, use a beveled washer.

The washer you install needs to fit the stem perfectly, so it's best to take the stem with you to your local hardware store. You can also buy a washer assortment kit. These kits usually include a variety of washer screws as well. Look for a kit with a dozen or more washer sizes.

When you've located the right washer, press it into the stem's retainer, and tighten the screw through it. Before returning the stem to its faucet port, lubricate the washer with heatproof or food-grade plumber's grease, available at hardware and plumbing outlets.

Replacing Faucet Seats

When the valve seat in a compression faucet appears pitted or feels rough, replace it if possible. New washers installed over damaged seats won't last long, and each subsequent leak will worsen the seat condition. Replacing a seat is not difficult, but finding a replacement can be time consuming.

First, determine whether the faucet has replaceable seats. Most kitchen and bathroom faucets do, but some tub faucets do not. Shutoff valves and hose bibcocks almost never have replaceable seats. To determine whether a seat is replaceable, use a flashlight to illuminate the inside of the faucet and look for a wrenching surface in the throat of the seat. If the inner surface of the inlet is hex shaped or has four deep grooves, the seat is replaceable. If it's smooth, the seat was machined into the faucet body and is not replaceable.

Removing the Seat. To remove a defective seat, you'll need a seat wrench—an inexpensive L-shaped tool with two tapered ends, one large and one small. The wrenching surface on some models is a continuous taper; on others, it's stepped, small to large. Both types work. Just insert one end of the wrench through the throat of the seat, and press down firmly. While bearing down on the wrench, rotate it in a counterclockwise direction. When the seat breaks free, spin it out. If a seat refuses to budge, position the wrench squarely in the seat and tap the wrench lightly with a hammer. The seat-to-faucet connection is brass to brass, so the seat should break free with little effort.

Faucet seats come in many shapes and sizes, so take the old one with you to a well-stocked plumbing store to be sure you get an exact replacement. The profile of the replacement may appear slightly different, but its threads, height, and rim size should match those of the seat you've removed. When you get it home, wedge the new seat onto the wrench and tighten it into the faucet port (photo at bottom right). Assuming the stem is in good condition, the new seat should give the faucet years of new life.

SMART TIP

"H" is for Left. The hot-side faucet handle, usually marked "H" somewhere on the handle, should always be on the left as you face the faucet. If it's not, the faucet may have been installed backward or the water lines under the sink may be reversed. To see whether the faucet was installed backward, check the stems. They may look alike, but they don't rotate the same. With compression faucets, you turn the water on by rotating the hot-water handle counterclockwise and the cold-water handle clockwise. If your faucet doesn't work that way, someone reversed the stems. A repair is your chance to correct them.

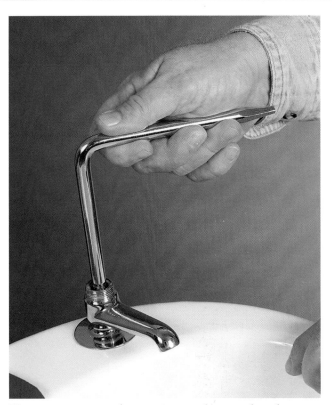

Use a seat wrench to remove a damaged replaceable faucet seat.

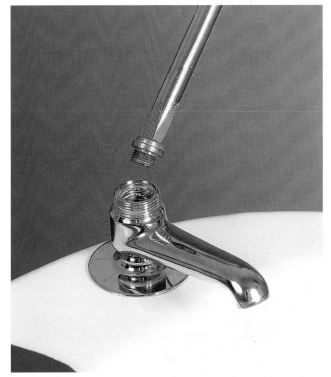

Slide the new seat onto the wrench, and install it in the faucet, turning clockwise.

Fixing Ball-Type Faucets

Delta Faucet Company is one of the pioneers in alternative faucet design, with its proprietary ball-and-cam mechanism, and actually offers two name brands. The Delta trademark is sold through professional plumbers, while the Peerless line is sold at the retail level. You'll notice slight cosmetic differences between the two lines, but both use the original ball-and-cam mechanism.

What traditional ball-type faucets have going for them are affordable repair parts. You don't usually discard the entire mechanism. Instead, you can replace only those parts that are worn, which in many cases are the springs and rubber seals. Several repair kits are available. Some include only the inlet springs and seals; some include seals, springs, and cam cover; and some include all mechanical components, including a stainless-steel or plastic control ball and a special wrench needed to remove the old ball.

How to Repair a Leaky Ball Faucet

To gain access to a ball-type sink faucet, turn off the water at the shut-off valves and tip up the handle. Loosen the Allen screw in the lower-front section of the handle, and lift off the handle. Where the handle had been, you'll find a large chrome cap with either wrenching surfaces or a knurled rim. If the nut you see has wrenching surfaces, loosen the nut with smooth-jaw pliers or an adjustable wrench. If the cap has a knurled rim, use either the Delta wrench that comes with each repair kit or large adjustable pliers padded with cloth or duct tape.

With the cap removed, lift the nylon and neoprene cam that covers the top of the ball. Then remove the ball. Set both aside. Reach into the faucet body, and using the Allen wrench or a small screwdriver, lift the cold-water rubber seal and its spring from the inlet port. Then lift the hot-water seal and spring. There's little noticeable difference between old and new seals and springs, so it's easy to get them mixed up. Throw out the old ones immediately. If you plan to replace the cam, discard it as well. If your faucet is more than 10 years old or has dripped for several months, replace the ball, too.

Reassembly. Assuming you'll be replacing everything except the ball, press each rubber seal onto its spring. Slide the seal and spring onto an Allen wrench or screwdriver, with the seal facing up. With an index finger holding the assembly in place, insert the spring and seal into the inlet. Install the remaining seal and spring in the same way.

With the new seals installed, press the ball into the body. The ball will have a peglike key on one side that matches a slot in the body, so there's no chance you'll get it wrong. Press the new cam cover over the ball, and align its key with the keyway on the faucet body. Push it down until the key engages, and then thread the cap over it. Tighten the cap until it feels snug, but don't overdo it. Replace the handle, and test your work. If the faucet drips or water appears around the handle, remove the handle and tighten the cap slightly.

Ball-Type Faucet Anatomy

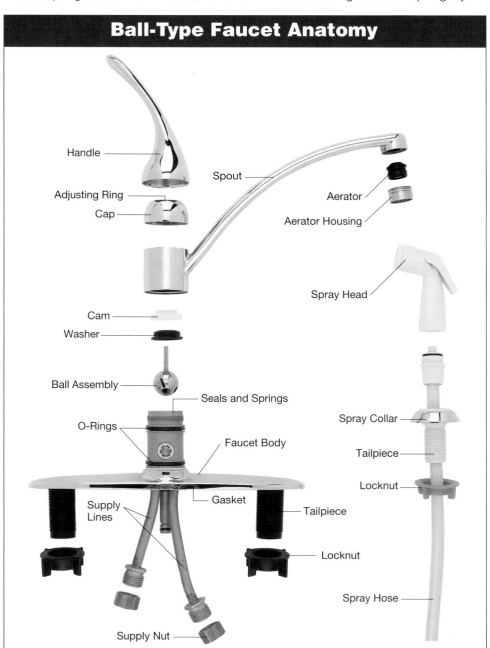

- Handle
- Spout
- Adjusting Ring
- Aerator
- Cap
- Aerator Housing
- Spray Head
- Cam
- Washer
- Ball Assembly
- Seals and Springs
- O-Rings
- Spray Collar
- Faucet Body
- Tailpiece
- Supply Lines
- Gasket
- Locknut
- Tailpiece
- Supply Nut
- Locknut
- Spray Hose

Repairing Ball-Type Faucets

1 To reach the handle screw, shut off the water and tip back the handle. Insert an Allen wrench or faucet tool, and remove the screw.

2 Loosen the cam nut to gain access to the ball assembly. Delta faucets have slotted nuts (inset); Peerless units have wrenching surfaces.

3 Lift the plastic cam to expose the ball assembly below. Plan at least to replace the cam and the faucet seals.

4 Lift the ball from the faucet body, and set it aside. Some kits come with replacement balls and some do not, so choose accordingly.

5 Use an Allen wrench or thin screwdriver to lift the rubber seals and springs from the inlet and outlet openings. Replace them all.

SMART TIP

Getting Rid of a Faucet Sprayer. If you don't use the faucet sprayer or it does not work correctly, you can remove and free up a sink deck hole for a hot-water or soap dispenser. You will need to close off the faucet nipple with a threaded cap. (Some nipples are threaded inside, so you can use a threaded plug to close it off.) Turn off the water; remove the hose spray; apply pipe joint compound to the faucet nipple threads; and tighten the plug or cap onto the nipple. Removing the sprayer not only opens up a hole in the sink deck, but it also removes the tubing required by the sprayer from under the sink.

6 Faucet Repairs

Repairing Cartridge Faucets

Repair of a cartridge-type faucet usually consists of merely replacing a long, self-contained cartridge.

Cartridge faucets offer an important benefit: if the water piping was installed backward, you can still have the hot water on the left. All you do to reverse the hot and cold sides is rotate the stem 180 degrees. This is a handy feature in back-to-back bathrooms, where a shared set of risers leaves one bath with reversed piping. A reversible faucet saves pipe and aggravation. But you must also make sure you replace the cartridge in the same orientation.

Repairing a Single-Handle Kitchen Faucet

Begin by turning off the water at the shutoff valves. The faucet handle may or may not have a chrome or plastic index cap. If it does, pry under the cap with a utility knife to gain access to the handle screw. If it doesn't, like the one shown in the photo, just pull off the cover.

Remove the screw from the handle, and tip the handle up and back. The handle's cam slot fits into a deep groove in the pivot nut, so expect to have to wiggle and coax it a bit. When the lever clears the pivot nut, lift it and its plastic hood from the faucet column. Loosen and remove the threaded pivot nut to reveal the top of the cartridge. Looking closely, you'll see that the cartridge is locked in place by a small U-shaped clip, positioned horizontally across the top of the cartridge. Use needle-nose pliers or a screwdriver to remove this clip. (inset). Then grasp the cartridge stem, and pull straight up. If it feels stuck, grip it with pliers and pull a little harder.

Replacing the Cartridge and Handle.
To make the repair, simply insert a new cartridge into the port, and press it down as far as it will go, aligning the flat notches in the stem with the brass-body slots. Insert the retainer clip. If it won't go in all the way, rotate the new cartridge locked in place, and thread the pivot. Push the clip into its slot until it bottoms out. With the new cartridge locked in place in the faucet, thread the pivot

nut back onto the column and replace the handle.

Replacing the handle can also be tricky. The cam opening in the handle must engage the groove of the pivot nut. If it doesn't, the handle won't operate through its full range. You'll be able to turn the water on and off, but just barely. To avoid the problem, tip up the handle as high as it will go within its plastic hood. Carefully engage the back of the lever in the pivot nut's groove. When you feel it engage, press the handle down, install the stem screw, and replace the decorative cover. Turn the water back on, and test your work. If you find that the hot water is now on the right side, remove the handle and rotate the stem 180 degrees.

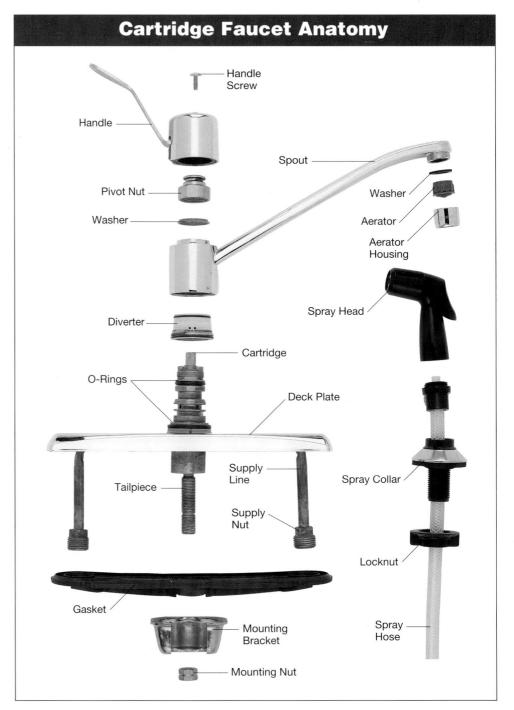

Cartridge Faucet Anatomy

- Handle Screw
- Handle
- Spout
- Pivot Nut
- Washer
- Washer
- Aerator
- Aerator Housing
- Spray Head
- Diverter
- Cartridge
- O-Rings
- Deck Plate
- Tailpiece
- Supply Line
- Supply Nut
- Spray Collar
- Locknut
- Gasket
- Mounting Bracket
- Spray Hose
- Mounting Nut

Repairing a Cartridge Faucet

1 To get access to the handle screw, lift the decorative cap from the column. If there's no lift-off cap, pry up the index cap.

2 Remove the handle screw using a Phillips-head screwdriver. The screw is threaded into the stem of the cartridge.

3 Lift the handle and hood from the faucet to reveal the pivot nut. The hood covers the top of the cartridge.

4 Use an adjustable wrench to remove the pivot nut. Rotate the nut counterclockwise to unscrew it from the faucet body.

5 Using needle-nose pliers, withdraw the retainer clip to remove the cartridge.

6 Lift out the cartridge by the stem.

Repairing Two-Handle Cartridge Faucets

Many manufacturers offer two-handle cartridge faucets, most often as low-cost alternatives to their single-control models. They are modestly priced and perfect for the mechanically timid because anyone can overhaul them.

To fix a leaking faucet, shut off the water and pry the index cap from the handle. Remove the handle, and loosen the cartridge nut using an adjustable wrench, smooth-jaw pliers, or groove-joint pliers with the jaws wrapped in duct tape. Lift the original cartridge from the faucet body; throw it away; and stick a new one in its place. Restore the nut and handle. Be sure to work on only one side at a time to keep from accidentally reversing the cartridges. When you're finished, turn on the water to test your work.

Most dual-handle cartridge faucets have disposable cartridges similar to those just described. But some have spring-loaded rubber seals in the inlet ports like those you find in ball-type single-handle faucets. If upon lifting the cartridge you notice these accessible seals, keep the cartridge and replace only the seals and springs.

If you find that your faucet cartridges are hard to remove, hard-water calcification over the years may have stuck them in place. Some faucet manufacturers offer cartridge extraction tools, but it also helps to pour warm vinegar into the faucet port and around the cartridge. Give the vinegar a few minutes to work, and try pulling the cartridge again.

Watch the Sleeve

Some cartridge faucets have a decorative sleeve over the cartridge. Remove the sleeve to reach the retaining clip.

Repairing a Two-Handle Cartridge Faucet

1 Use a knife to pry the index cap from the handle. ("Hot" should be on the left.) Then remove the retaining screw, and lift off the handle.

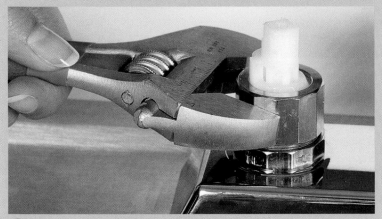

2 Using an adjustable wrench, turn the chrome retaining nut counterclockwise to remove it from the cartridge.

3 Lift out the old cartridge, and install an exact replacement. Before inserting the new cartridge, lubricate the O-rings with plumber's grease.

Repairing Ceramic-Disk Faucets

Ceramic-disk faucets are particularly vulnerable to sediment accumulations. For this reason, don't assume that a dripping faucet needs a complete overhaul. When a ceramic-disk faucet develops a steady drip, remove the aerator and move the handle through all positions several times. If sediment was the culprit, this should clear it. In general, a ceramic-disk faucet is not a good choice if you experience sediment problems with your water, especially if they are so severe that you require a filter.

Fixing a Leak in a Ceramic-Disk Faucet

If you have a newer-style ceramic-disk faucet and you can't seem to clear the sediment by rotating the handle, you'll need to check the cartridge. Shut off the water, tip back the handle, and loosen the setscrew. Remove the handle, and lift off the decorative cartridge cap. Use a small flat-blade screwdriver to remove the retaining screws. Then lift the cartridge from the faucet. If you see sediment in the inlet ports, clean it out using tweezers. You can also remove the neoprene seals (visible in photo 3) to look for sediment. Clean them if you find sediment, but if you don't find any, the problem is likely in the cartridge. Most ceramic cartridges are not serviceable, so replace the cartridge, and reinstall the handle.

Clearing Sediment Buildup

Mineral-encrusted aerators are easy to unscrew from the faucet spout for cleaning or replacement.

Soak the scaled-over aerator parts in vinegar, and clear the screens with a straightened paper clip.

Fixing a Leak in a Ceramic-Disk Faucet

1 To locate the handle screw, shut off the water and tip the handle back. Use an Allen wrench to remove the screw.

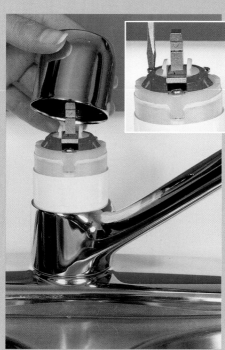

2 Lift off the decorative cap to expose the cartridge. Using a flat-blade screwdriver, loosen the screws at the top of the cartridge (inset).

3 Look for sediment near either or both of the inlet ports. Clear the sediment and clean the seals, or replace the cartridge.

tubs & showers

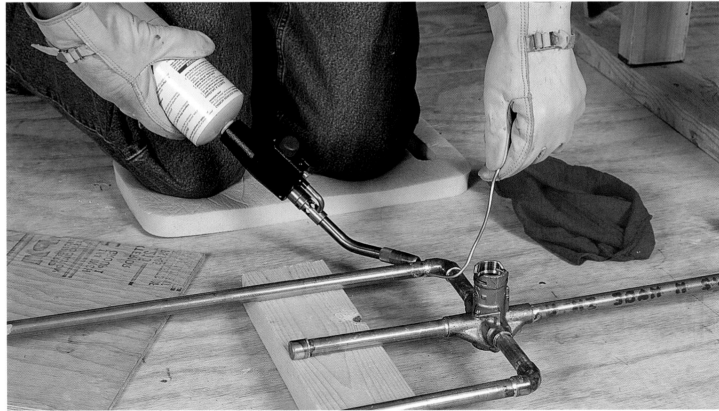

Tub and Shower Drains and Faucets

Tubs and showers have the look of permanence, enough so that when they wear out, many homeowners are reluctant to replace them.

But they're *not* permanent, and they're not that difficult to repair or replace. Acrylic and fiberglass prefabricated units make the installation of a shower or tub fairly straightforward. Newer tubs are lighter than their cast-iron ancestors are. And there's no real mystery behind faucets and drains.

The hardest part of the job may be the wall and ceiling finishing you will have to do (or have done by a drywall contractor) when you've replaced or fixed the units.

Bathtub Outlet Anatomy

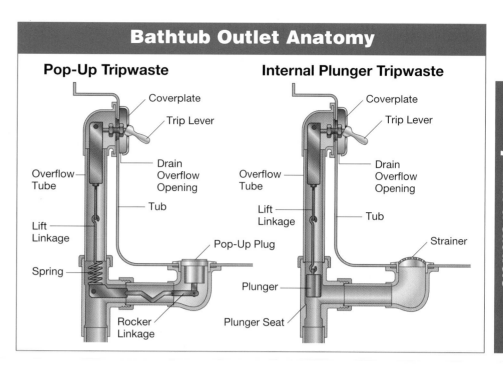

Pop-Up Tripwaste

- Coverplate
- Trip Lever
- Overflow Tube
- Drain Overflow Opening
- Tub
- Lift Linkage
- Spring
- Pop-Up Plug
- Rocker Linkage

Internal Plunger Tripwaste

- Coverplate
- Trip Lever
- Overflow Tube
- Drain Overflow Opening
- Lift Linkage
- Tub
- Strainer
- Plunger
- Plunger Seat

Bathtub Installation Anatomy

There are five types of bathtubs: enameled cast iron, porcelain-coated steel, plastic-coated porcelain steel, fiberglass, and acrylic. A tub drain and faucet should be installed in the same wall, so order your tub accordingly. Standard tubs are 60 inches long, but special-order tubs are available in lengths from 48 to 72 inches. Jetted tubs are available in a variety of sizes and shapes.

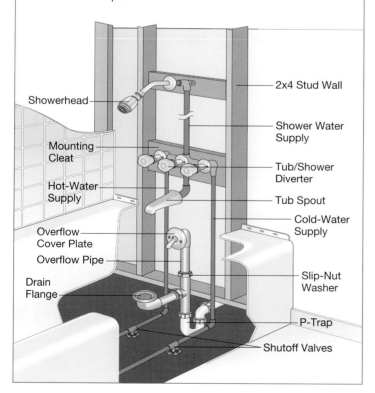

- Showerhead
- Mounting Cleat
- Hot-Water Supply
- Overflow Cover Plate
- Overflow Pipe
- Drain Flange
- 2x4 Stud Wall
- Shower Water Supply
- Tub/Shower Diverter
- Tub Spout
- Cold-Water Supply
- Slip-Nut Washer
- P-Trap
- Shutoff Valves

Shower Installation Anatomy

You can build a custom shower any size you want, but those built from components start with a plastic or fiberglass shower pan that measures from 32 x 32 inches up to 40 x 60 inches. You can also find shower pans that fit into corners.

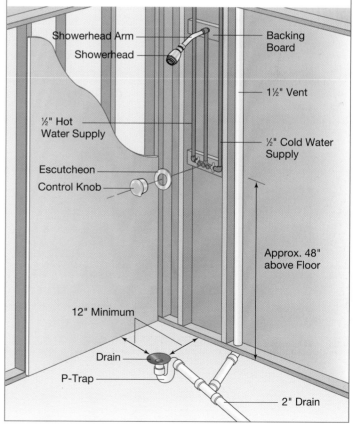

- Showerhead Arm
- Showerhead
- Backing Board
- 1½" Vent
- ½" Hot Water Supply
- ½" Cold Water Supply
- Escutcheon
- Control Knob
- Approx. 48" above Floor
- 12" Minimum
- Drain
- P-Trap
- 2" Drain

Fixing Single-Handle Tub and Shower Faucets

1 To gain access to the handle screw, start by removing the handle's decorative index cap. Pry under it using a knife.

2 Use a Phillips-head screwdriver to remove the handle. Be careful not to lose the plastic inset bushing.

3 Carefully pull the decorative stainless-steel inner sleeve from the valve body and trim plate. Use needle-nose pliers to pull the U-shape retaining clip from the cartridge (inset), being careful not to bend it.

4 Pull the old cartridge from the faucet, and install an exact replacement. Replace the retaining clip, inner sleeve, and handle.

SMART TIP

Escutcheon Alternative. Deep-set escutcheons use two mounting designs. In one, a knurled nut just under the faucet handle keeps the escutcheon in place. In the other, the escutcheon has internal threads and is turned directly onto the faucet stem. If you don't see a nut when you remove the faucet handle, grip the escutcheon directly using your hand or, if it's tight, smooth-jaw pliers or a strap wrench to remove it. Faucet escutcheons without retaining nuts usually have internal threads. They just twist off.

Working with Scald-Control Faucets

Scald-control faucets have long been installed in hospitals and nursing homes, and in the past few years many codes have been updated to require scald control for residential bath and shower faucets. It takes only a couple of seconds of exposure to 140-degree-F water to produce a third-degree burn—and only one second at 150 degrees F. Many homeowners have their water heaters set that high. (A 125-degree-F setting is safer, and your heater will give you longer service at that setting.) Small children, the elderly, and anyone with limited mobility are at greatest risk.

Every manufacturer now makes affordable scald-control faucets for residential use.

Handle-Rotation Stop. Scald control is delivered in two ways. First is a temperature-limit adjustment, in the form of a handle-rotation stop. With a handle stop, you remove the handle and dial in a comfortable water temperature, with the water running, and then lock the setting and replace the handle. Thereafter, when you turn the handle to "Hot," it will rotate only to the stop position. You can reduce the temperature with cold water, but you can't exceed the hot limit. Because ground temperatures change with the seasons, you may need to adjust these settings twice a year.

Pressure-Balance Spool. The second mechanism, a pressure-balance spool, is designed to accommodate a sudden drop in pressure on one side of the piping system. Pressure drops are common. The most familiar scenario: you're taking a shower when someone in an adjacent bathroom flushes the toilet. The toilet diverts half the line pressure from the cold side of the faucet, upsetting the ratio of hot-to-cold water. The result is a sudden blast of hot water.

Balance spools come in several forms, but the most common is a perforated cylinder with a similarly perforated internal slide. The slightest drop in line pressure on one side of the faucet moves the slide over a bit, realigning the perforations and reducing intake from the high-pressure side. When pressure is restored to the weak side, the slide returns to its original position. These simple devices are so effective that water won't even flow through a faucet when one side is turned off. You'll find pressure-balance spools in two locations. Some are built into the faucet body—with front access—and some are built into the valve cartridge.

As an added benefit, many of these upgraded faucets are built with integral stops, one on each side of the control. Instead of shutting down the entire water system for repairs, you can just close the stops using a screwdriver.

Cleaning Sediment from a Pressure-Balance Spool

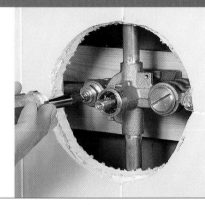

Some scald-control faucets have integral water stops. Use a screwdriver to shut off the water.

To clear a balancing spool of sediment, pull it out and tap it on the counter. Flush the spool with water, and replace it.

Pressure-Balanced Cartridges

Scald-control measures have changed the way you work on familiar cartridge faucets. Many cartridges and faucets look like standard units, but they now contain a balancing spool, and they are installed differently. You can't remove them from the faucet without a special tool, so don't try pulling them out, the way you would a standard cartridge. Either buy a metal twist tool, like the one shown here, or use the little tool that comes with each replacement cartridge. If you need to work on one of these faucets, proceed carefully until you learn how things work. Manufacturers normally provide toll-free numbers and Web sites with their instructions.

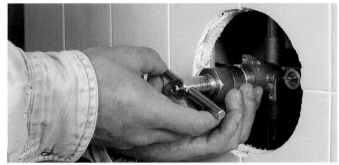

Cartridges with built-in balancing spools often require a special removal tool.

Replacing a Tub Drain Assembly

1 Begin by unscrewing the tripwaste cover plate and pulling the tripwaste linkage from the overflow.

2 Unscrew the drain fitting.

5 Stick plumber's putty to the drain flange.

6 Screw the spud into the drain shoe and gasket while a helper holds them in place.

9 Pull the plastic trap down far enough to allow you to screw the tailpiece into the drain T-fitting. Coat the threads using pipe joint compound.

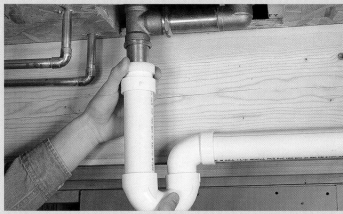

10 Slip the compression nut and washer onto the tailpiece, and tighten the nut to secure the tailpiece in the trap riser.

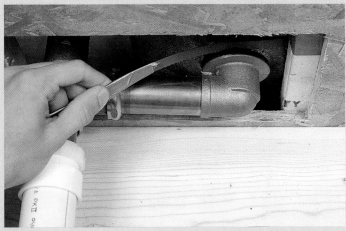

3 If you can't free the old drain spud nut, cut through it using a hacksaw blade or a reciprocating saw with a metal-cutting blade.

4 Loosen the trap connection to free the overflow tube. Expect to find a friction washer or compression washer.

7 Install the rubber gasket on the bathtub overflow tube, and slide the tube upward into the wall cavity from below.

8 Join the drain and overflow pipes in the drain T-fitting, and tighten all the nuts using large groove-joint pliers.

11 From inside the tub, slip the tripwaste linkage into the overflow tube until the cover plate sits against the tube's gasket, and secure the plate.

SMART TIP

Tub and Shower Drain Access. If you want to replace an inaccessible drain (that is, when the tub is installed on a concrete slab or above a finished ceiling below), you'll need to do the work through the back of the plumbing wall. If your tub has an access panel already in place behind the tub, you're in luck. If not, you'll need to create one. To gain access, cut out the drywall between the two studs that straddle the center of the tub. When you've finished the installation, you can either patch the drywall or install a permanent access cover. For hidden areas, you can purchase a ready-made plastic panel.

Replacing a Faucet

The faucet connection methods will be dictated by the kind of unit you buy: whether it's a single- or dual-control model; whether it has union fittings, threaded ports, or soldered joints; and so on. If your piping is made of galvanized steel, you'll also need to consider the problem of electrolytic corrosion, which results when you join copper and steel piping directly.

If direct copper-to-steel connections are not a problem in your area, begin by threading galvanized-steel couplings onto each riser, using pipe-thread sealing tape. (It's a good idea to use couplings, with their female ports, because copper stretches when threaded over steel, often enough to cause a leak.) As always, be sure to use a second wrench to backhold the supply pipes when tightening the new fittings. With the steel couplings in place, wrap three rounds of pipe-sealing tape counterclockwise over the threads of two copper male adapters, and tighten the adapters into the couplings.

If you had to cut the old steel shower riser to remove the faucet, you'll have to install a new one. There are several options. You can remove the old riser and fish Type L soft copper in its place through the faucet opening, uncoiling the pipe as you go. This requires cutting a second opening at showerhead level. If the basement ceiling beneath the tub is open, you can usually install rigid piping from below. In any case, solder a drop-eared elbow to the top of the pipe, and feed it into the wall. Screw the elbow to a backing board.

With a new shower riser ready, solder copper inlet stubs into the side ports of the valve. The easiest approach is to make them a little long, then hold the faucet in place and measure between the stubs and the copper adapters on the supply tubes. Cut these lengths, and test-fit the riser-to-faucet connections.

With the faucet temporarily connected to the supply tubes and shower riser, cut stubs for the tub spout. If your new spout is threaded, solder a ½-inch-diameter male adapter to the end of the horizontal pipe so that the threads of the adapter protrude through the finished tub wall about ½ inch. If the spout clamps onto the pipe with an Allen screw, bring the copper pipe through the wall about 3 inches.

When you have all of the pieces fitted, pull the assembly apart and flux the ends of the stubs. Before soldering, remove the faucet cartridge or stem to keep from warping the plastic components.

Solder as much of the assembly as possible outside the wall. Insert the stubs into the faucet ports; lay the faucet on the floor; and solder each joint carefully. After the valve cools, flux the remaining joints; connect the faucet to the in-wall piping; and solder these joints. When the faucet cools, reassemble it and turn the water on to test your work. Repair the wall and install the spout, showerhead, and faucet trim.

Replacing a Tub-Shower Faucet

1 If you'd like to save the old spout, use a strap wrench to unscrew it from the faucet and avoid damaging the finish.

4 Loosen the faucet unions using a pipe wrench, and lift out and discard the old faucet. Remove and discard the unions.

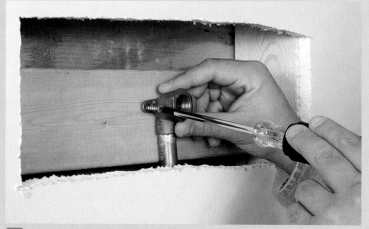

7 When adding piping for the showerhead, cut an opening in the wall to secure the drop-eared elbow to blocking.

2 With the spout and escutcheons removed, use a grout saw to strip the grout from the tiles in the removal area.

3 Start near the spout or faucet stems, and carefully pry each tile away from the wall. Set the tiles aside for reuse.

5 Apply pipe-thread sealing tape, and then thread ½-in. galvanized couplings to the old faucet supply tubes. Or attach new couplings to copper tubing and go to step 7.

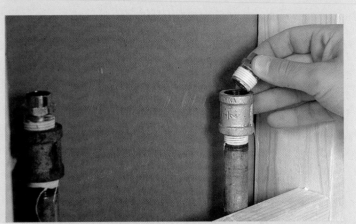

6 Using pipe-thread sealing tape (not pipe joint compound), screw ½-in. copper male adapters into the couplings.

8 Complete the new faucet piping in copper. Install the spout pipe so that the spout will be 6 in. below the faucet body when installed.

9 Remove the nylon faucet cartridge from the faucet body, and sweat all copper fittings using lead-free solder.

water heaters

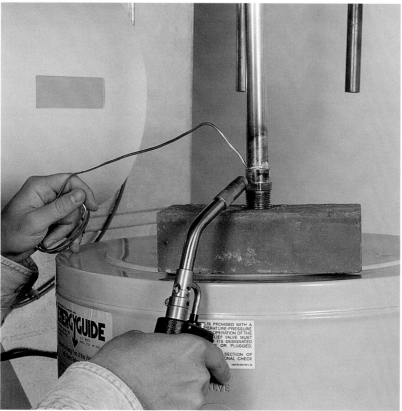

Electric & Gas Water Heaters

Conventional tank heaters are basic-technology appliances, though these days they are more efficient than they used to be. Because of their no-frills mechanics, they are the most affordable and most popular heaters sold today.

Electric Water Heaters

An electric water heater consists of a welded steel inner tank covered by insulation and a metal outer cabinet. The inner surface of the steel tank is coated with a furnace-fired porcelain lining, often described as a glass lining. The bottom of the tank is slightly convex, which helps to control sediment, and a drain valve sits just above the bottom of the tank. The top of the tank has two water fittings and sometimes a separate anode fitting. The top (or upper side) of the heater also contains a fitting for a temperature-and-pressure (T&P) relief valve.

Two resistance-heat electrodes, called elements, heat the water in the tank. Each element is controlled by its own thermostat. The thermostats are joined electrically so that the elements can be energized in sequence: the bottom element comes on only when the top one shuts off. The elements are threaded or bolted into the unit, and the thermostats are surface-mounted next to the elements, covered by access panels and insulation. To help keep the tank from rusting, a magnesium anode rod is installed through the top of the heater. And finally, a dip tube usually hangs from the inlet fitting and delivers incoming water to the bottom of the tank.

Plastic Tanks. Electric water heaters with plastic tanks carry a lifetime warranty and cost about double the price of standard water heaters. Plastic makes an ideal tank because it can't corrode. In hard-water situations, steel-tank heaters tend to accumulate precipitated minerals, shortening service life. Sediment can be a problem in plastic heaters, but it's more manageable: they have rounded bottoms with large, centered drain plugs for easy draining. Plastic tanks are also highly insulated with non-ozone-depleting foam insulation. Along with better insulation comes lower fuel costs. You can earn back the price difference of these units in five to ten years.

Gas-Fired Water Heaters

A gas-fired water heater is like an electric unit in many respects (glazed tank, anode rod, dip tube, relief valve), but its open-flame heating components require design differences. A flue tube runs through the center of the tank, from bottom to top. Viewed from above, the tank looks like a donut. To capture latent exhaust-gas heat, a wavy steel damper is suspended in the flue like a ribbon. The bottom of the tank is convex, which helps send sediment to the outer edges and away from the area just above the burner. At the bottom of the heater is the circular burner, and at the top, the exhaust-gas flue hat.

Gas goes to the burner through a thermostatically triggered control valve mounted on the lower front of the heater. The burner is joined to the control valve by three tubes. The largest of the tubes is the main gas feed. The mid-size tube is the pilot-gas feed, and the smallest is the thermocouple lead. A thermocouple is little more than a copper wire with an expansion plug controlling the gas valve at one end and a heat sensor at the other. The heat from the flame sends a millivolt of electricity to the expansion plug, which holds the gas control valve open.

Water Heater Anatomy

Electric

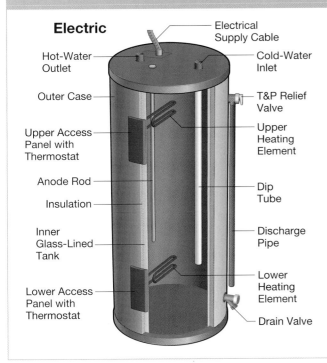

- Hot-Water Outlet
- Electrical Supply Cable
- Cold-Water Inlet
- Outer Case
- T&P Relief Valve
- Upper Access Panel with Thermostat
- Upper Heating Element
- Anode Rod
- Dip Tube
- Insulation
- Inner Glass-Lined Tank
- Discharge Pipe
- Lower Access Panel with Thermostat
- Lower Heating Element
- Drain Valve

Gas

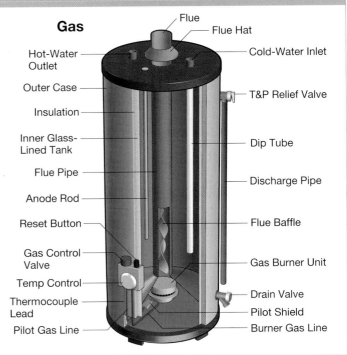

- Flue
- Flue Hat
- Hot-Water Outlet
- Cold-Water Inlet
- Outer Case
- T&P Relief Valve
- Insulation
- Inner Glass-Lined Tank
- Dip Tube
- Flue Pipe
- Discharge Pipe
- Anode Rod
- Flue Baffle
- Reset Button
- Gas Control Valve
- Gas Burner Unit
- Temp Control
- Thermocouple Lead
- Drain Valve
- Pilot Shield
- Pilot Gas Line
- Burner Gas Line

Common Water-Heater Problems

You will generally come across just a few main problems with a water heater: a faulty T&P relief valve, accumulation of sediment in the bottom of the tank, and a corroded anode rod.

Faulty T&P Relief Valves

A temperature-and-pressure (T&P) relief valve is a water heater's primary safety device. Should a thermostat stick and the heater not shut off, the resulting increase in heat and pressure would be relieved through the T&P valve. Otherwise, the heater could explode.

The problem with T&P valves is that you can't always tell when they are no longer working. A leaky valve may signal a defect, but just as often, it indicates that the valve is working just as it should. A temporary pressure surge elsewhere in the system may have been relieved through the T&P valve.

The best way to know for sure is to keep track of when the water appears. If it only happens when you do laundry, for example, your washer solenoid, which can produce substantial back-shock in the water system when it abruptly shuts off the water flow to the machine, is the likely culprit. (See "Water-Hammer Arrestors," on page 98.)

Replacing a T&P Relief Valve. It's good practice to test your water heater's T&P valve every six months or so. Just lift the test lever and let it snap back (inset photo below, left). This should produce a momentary blast of hot water through the valve's overflow tube. If no water appears or if the lever won't budge, replace the valve immediately. If water does appear but you notice that the valve now drips steadily, your test probably deposited flakes of scale in the valve seat. This scale will often clear itself if you open and close the valve several times. If it doesn't, tap lightly on the lever pin with a hammer and then retest. If it still leaks, the

SMART TIP

Top-Mounted and Replacement T&P Valves.
If your water heater's T&P relief valve is threaded into the top of the unit, you may need to cut the overflow pipe to remove it. After you've installed the new valve, reconnect the old overflow pipe, using a soldered coupling or compression coupling to repair the cut. If your old valve was without an overflow pipe, install one. Run it to within 6 inches of the floor. When buying a replacement T&P valve, be sure that it has a pressure rating lower than that of the water heater. If your heater is rated at 175 psi, as noted on its service tag, buy a valve that is rated at 150 psi. Local codes may specify a pressure rating.

best course of action is to replace the valve.

To replace a T&P relief valve, shut off the water and power and let the water cool for at least a few hours. Open an upstairs faucet and the tank's drain valve. You won't need to empty the entire tank, just drain it to a point below the valve fitting. The T&P valve may be mounted on the top or in the side of your heater. In either case, remove the overflow pipe from its outlet. Then use a pipe wrench to unscrew the old valve from the tank (photo below, left). Coat the new valve's threads using pipe-thread sealing tape or pipe joint compound, and tighten it into the heater (photo below, right). Stop when the valve's outlet points straight down. Screw the overflow pipe into the valve's outlet, and turn the water back on. Bleed all air from the tank through an upstairs faucet, and turn the power back on.

If the new valve also spills water, the water heater's thermostat is sticking. Either replace the unit or call a professional plumber to replace the control valve.

Replacing a T&P Valve

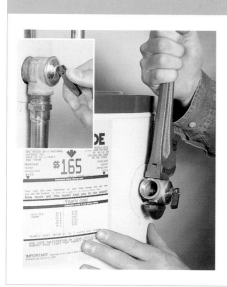

Test the T&P valve periodically (inset), and remove it if it seizes up or doesn't seem to work properly.

Wrap pipe-thread sealing tape around the threads of the new valve, and tighten it into the opening in the water heater.

Changing an Anode Rod

Even though steel water-heater tanks are lined with a vitrified porcelain finish, the coating process is far from perfect. In fact, every glass lining has dozens of tiny pinholes where rust can start. The tank could rust through were it not for its sacrificial anode rod.

An anode rod works by sacrificing itself to corrosion, thereby preventing the tank from corroding. Most metals corrode, but at different rates. Water-heater anode rods are typically made of magnesium because it corrodes at a faster rate than does iron. As the magnesium corrodes, it sheds electrons, which migrate to the pinholes in the lining. This electron-rich environment keeps the tank from rusting. It takes four to five years for an anode to fail; thus, the five-year tank warranty. Ten-year heaters have larger anodes or two anodes. It's a good idea to replace the anode rod at the end of the warranty period.

1 Use a breaker bar and 1¹⁄₁₆-in. socket wrench to break the top nut of the anode rod free. Unscrew it, and lift the rod out.

2 This five-year anode rod has exceeded its service life and must be replaced.

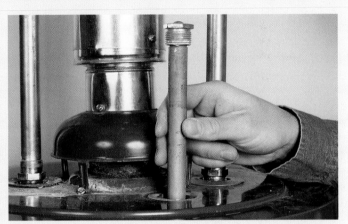

3 Use just a little pipe joint compound on the threads of the top nut, and tighten the new anode rod in place.

Replacing a Sediment-Clogged Drain Valve

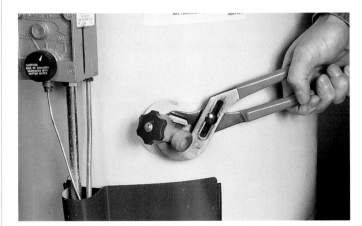

Remove the leaky old drain valve using large groove-joint pliers.

Install a new valve, turning it clockwise. Use pipe-thread sealing tape or pipe joint compound on the threads.

Servicing Gas-Fired Water Heaters

Gas-fired water heaters have service needs that are different from those for electric units. You may experience problems with the combustion process, the vent pipe, the burner itself, or the thermocouple and pilot.

Combustion-Air Problems

If your gas-fired water heater makes a puffing sound at the burner, it's not getting enough air. Air shortages are especially common in utility rooms, where a water heater, furnace, and clothes dryer all compete for air. Allow the water heater to run for a few minutes with the utility-room door closed. When it starts puffing, open the door and a nearby window. If the flame settles into smooth operation, inadequate combustion air was the culprit. Either cut a large vent through the utility-room wall or replace the solid door with a louvered door.

Vent-Pipe Problems

When a gas-fired water heater runs, it creates a thermal draft, in which air from the room is also drawn up the flue. If there is insufficient secondary air or if the flue is partially clogged, deadly carbon monoxide gas may spill into your living space. Because carbon monoxide is odorless and invisible, it pays to test the efficiency of the flue from time to time. You can call your gas company for a sophisticated test, but the following method works. If the utility room has a door, close it. Wait a few minutes for the heater to develop a good draft, and then hold a smoking match, incense stick, or candle about 1 inch from the flue hat at the top of the heater (photo above, right). If the flue draws in the smoke, all is well. If the smoke is not drawn in or is pushed away from the flue, there's a problem. To determine

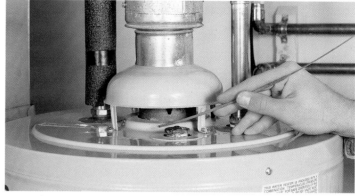

Use the smoke from a match, incense stick, or cigarette to test the flue.

whether the problem is an air-starved room or a clogged flue, repeat the procedure with a door and window open. If the smoke is now drawn into the flue, make the corrections noted in "Combustion-Air Problems," at left. If the flue still does not pull the smoke, call in a professional to inspect it.

Maintaining the Thermocouple and Burner

The job of the thermocouple is to hold the gas valve open so that gas can flow to the burner and pilot. If the pilot on your gas-fired water heater goes out and the heater goes out again after you re-light the pilot, the thermocouple is probably misaligned or defective.

Before buying a new thermocouple, check to see whether the existing thermocouple's sensor is positioned directly in the path of the pilot flame. If not, bend the fastener clip so that the pilot flame surrounds the sensor. Then light the pilot to see whether it keeps burning. If not, a new thermocouple is in order.

Water Hammer Arrestors

If you hear a pounding noise in your water system and see an occasional spill of water near your water heater, you have a water-hammer problem. Water-hammer arrestors have internal rubber bladders that act as shock absorbers for high-pressure back-shocks. You typically install them between the water piping and fixture. For a clothes washer, screw the arrestors onto the stop valves and the hoses onto the arrestors.

To stop T&P valve leaks, install water-hammer arrestors on the washing machine shutoffs.

Clean the Burner. As combustion gases degrade the inner surface of the water heater, flakes of rusty metal may fall onto the burner. The rust can cover gas jets around the burner's perimeter. With some jets blocked, the rest will flame orange and high, signaling a loss in efficiency.

Check the burner for rust as part of your routine maintenance. With the heater turned to pilot, remove the outer and inner access panels at the base of the heater. Shine a flashlight onto the burner. If you see rust on top of the burner, vacuum it off. Then turn on the water heater. If some of the gas openings still appear clogged, you'll have to remove the burner to clear them out. To do so, turn off the gas and loosen the nuts securing the three burner tubes to the gas control valve. Slide out the burner, and poke through the openings with a piece of wire.

Replace the Thermocouple. If you need to replace the thermocouple, pull the sensor from its clip. (Some are held in place by a screw.) Take the old thermocouple to a hardware store, and buy a matching one. Connect the new thermocouple, making sure that the sensor will catch the pilot flame. Reinstall the burner, and reconnect the burner tubes to the control valve.

To re-light the water heater, press down on the pilot button and hold it down for 30 seconds before lighting a match held using needle-nose pliers. Feed the flame into the heater. If the pilot goes out when you let up on the button, repeat the procedure. You may need to do this several times for the gas to push all the air from the pilot feed line. When the pilot stays on, replace the access panels and turn the control knob to "On."

Maintaining the Burner and Thermocouple

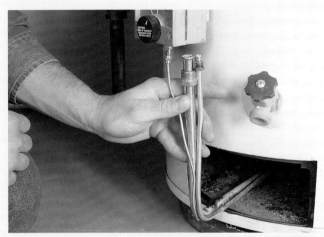

1 Loosen the three connecting nuts, and remove the burner assembly. Tip the assembly down and out.

2 While you have the burner out, ream its jets using a piece of wire. Also, vacuum any rust from the floor of the water heater.

3 Snap the new thermocouple into the burner, and secure the clip. If the thermocouple wire is too long, coil it.

4 Tighten all connections.

clearing drainpipes

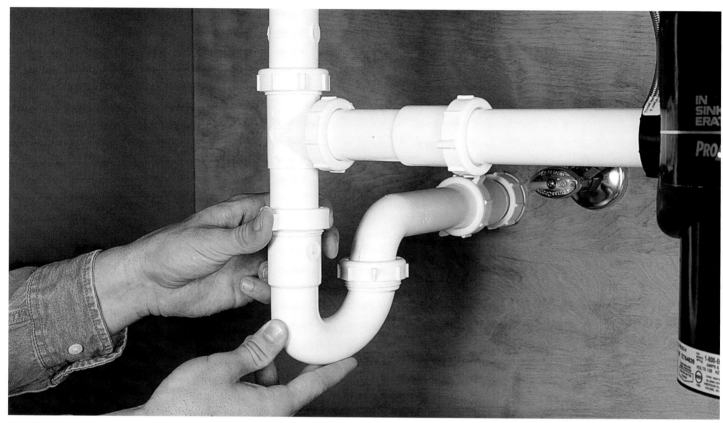

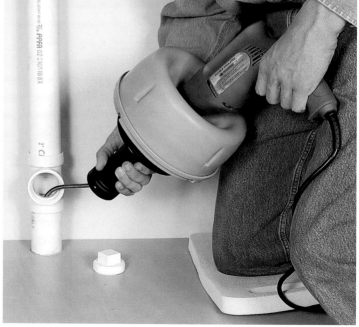

Drain Cleaners

When you're faced with a stopped-up drain, you'll need to clear it, either by breaking it down and dissolving it chemically or by mechanically removing the obstruction with a drain-clearing tool.

Chemical Drain Cleaners

There are three general varieties of chemically based drain cleaners: alkaline, enzymatic, and acidic.

Alkaline Cleaners. Supermarket products, which you pour directly into a stopped sink or tub, are alkali-based products. These have copper sulfide, sodium hydroxide, or sodium hypochloride as their active ingredients. They work on the simplest of hair and grease clogs, but they'll do little to clear an extended accumulation.

Enzymatic Cleaners. A less hazardous and more environmentally friendly version of drain cleaners uses enzymes to break down clogs. Enzymatic treatments often work, but they take a few days. They are especially good at preventive maintenance. Using an enzymatic drain treatment twice a year will help keep drains clear and will benefit your septic system if your house is not connected to a municipal sewer system.

Acidic Cleaners. Acids, the final group of chemical cleaners, are more troublesome. They can be effective, but they're enormously dangerous in the wrong hands. Sulfuric and hydrochloric acid will dissolve just about any blockage material commonly found in plumbing systems, including dish rags, diapers, chicken bones, and the like.

However, hydrochloric acid will also damage porcelain, most metals, and just about everything except vitreous china. Sulfuric acid is less likely to damage metal piping but will degrade aluminum, stainless steel, and porcelain. Its rotten-egg stench will also drive you from your home. These are products of last resort, so read labels and proceed extremely carefully. Avoid using them if at all possible.

Mechanical Drain Cleaners

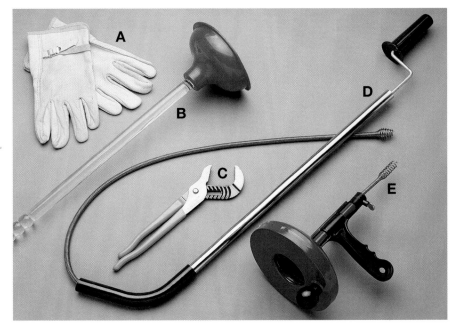

(A) work gloves, **(B)** plunger, **(C)** groove-joint pliers, **(D)** closet auger, **(E)** drain auger

Mechanical Drain Cleaners

Mechanically clearing a clogged drain or cleaning a slow-running one is not complex work and doesn't require an armful of tools. Using a plunger, a screwdriver, and a piece of wire, you'll be able to handle the most common clogs. For those rare occasions where a plunger doesn't seem to work, you'll need additional tools.

Plunger. Get the kind of plunger that has a foldout extension cup. When folded in, it works on sinks, showers, and tubs. When folded out, it fits a toilet outlet.

Drain Auger. A drain auger is a long coiled-wire cable with a springlike head on its working end. You'll see two kinds when you go shopping: one is just a coil of cable with a piece of offset tubing as a crank; the other has its cable spooled in a metal or plastic housing. Buy the one with the housing because its wider cranking arc provides better torque for stubborn clogs. The housing also minimizes the spraying of indelible black drain slime.

Closet Auger. A closet auger is also a drain snake, but its design limits its use to toilets (also known as water closets.) It consists of a 3-foot metal tube that bends at a right angle at the bottom. The tube houses a cable and crank-rod, which total about 6 feet. You insert the bend of the auger into the toilet outlet with the rod pulled back, then push the rod and cable forward while cranking in a clockwise direction.

Power Auger. If you try clearing a problem drain with a plunger or lightweight cable but don't seem to make much progress, you're probably dealing with an extended accumulation. Years of accumulation require a heavier cable with a more aggressive head. The head may be shaped like an arrowhead, or it may have caliper-like blades. Most such snakes are power-driven by either a hand-held drill-like motor or a chassis-mounted motor. There are two basic sizes. The light-duty ones are designed for drains up to about 2 inches in diameter. The larger heavy-duty ones are designed for sewers. These machines are rental items.

Clearing Techniques

Drain-cleaning tools are not particularly difficult to use. Knowing how to apply a few special techniques, however, makes them more effective.

Getting the Most from a Plunger

A plunger works better when you add water. Many slow-draining fixtures already have water in them, of course (that's how you know they're slow), but if yours doesn't, add some. In addition, make sure that all overflow tubes are blocked. If you don't block these passages, they'll bleed off the pressure created by the plunger.

When plunging a tub, hold a wet rag firmly against the bottom of the overflow plate. With bath basins, stuff a rag into the overflow openings just below the rim. Hold it firmly in place. The same goes for dual-compartment kitchen sinks. When plunging one side, plug the other. But when a sink compartment with a waste-disposal unit backs up,

plunge only that side. The problem here is usually a blocked T-fitting in the waste kit just under the sink.

Remember that suction is almost as effective as pressure, so try to maintain a good seal between the plunger and fixture surface through both the up and down motions. If the plunger doesn't seem to be creating enough pressure or suction because of the contour of the fixture, try coating the rim of the plunger with petroleum jelly. Follow every plunging by running hot water for at least a minute or two.

Effective Auger Techniques

Once you've gained access to the drainpipe, pull about 18 inches of cable from the spool and feed it carefully into the line.

Some drains reveal their clogs immediately. As soon as you pull the trap, you'll see it. Other lines appear clean but are clogged somewhere downstream. If you see no apparent obstruction, don't bother cranking the cable into the line. Just feed it in until you feel resistance. At this point,

Plunging to the Max

When plunging a tub, plug the overflow fitting with a wet rag.

When plunging a bathroom sink, cover the overflow hole in the basin with a wet rag.

Clearing Toilet Drains

To clear a toilet clog, first use a plunger that has a fold-out cup.

Use a closet auger if you can't clear a clogged toilet using a plunger.

Pry up the drain screen with a knife or flat-blade screwdriver if it is not held in place by screws.

Insert an auger cable directly into the trap, and turn the handle clockwise as you feed the cable.

Remove a bathroom sink's trap and trap arm, and feed the auger cable directly into the drainage line. Follow with plenty of hot water once you've reassembled the trap.

SMART TIP

Keep on Course. When you feed an auger cable into a T-fitting in a wall, use a flashlight and make sure the head of the cable points down. Be careful, because it's easy to send the cable in the wrong direction, up a vent pipe. Professional-quality drain augers are fitted with drop heads, which automatically seek the lowest route, but most do-it-yourself homeowner augers are not.

tighten the setscrew and push the cable forward while cranking in a steady, clockwise direction. (See the photo opposite.) When you run out of cable, loosen the setscrew, pull another 12 to 18 inches from the spool, tighten the setscrew, and crank forward again. Repeat this procedure until you break through the clog or reach the next-largest drainpipe. (You'll feel the cable flop around in the larger pipe.)

Meeting the Clog. You will know that you've snagged or forced open a clog when you feel the resistance—or lack of it—in the cable. This is an important consideration, especially with rented power equipment. With motor-driven cables, it's easy to break the cable off in the line when the head snags an obstruction. Always proceed slowly. When you feel sudden resistance followed by the sensation that you've broken through it, retrieve the line completely. This suggests that you've snagged an object, such as a rag. (In a sewer line, this behavior may indicate that you've hooked a bundle of threadlike tree roots.)

To retrieve a foreign object, pull the cable out of the line 1 or 2 feet at a time, feeding the cable into the spool as you go. As you pull back, continue cranking in a clockwise direction. Reversing direction will only release whatever you've snagged.

Push and Pull. If you feel a steady, prolonged resistance after first hitting the clog, try a push-and-pull approach. Push the cable forward 3 feet, then back 2 feet, then forward 4 feet, then back 2 feet, and so on. Stop if you feel the cable flip over when pushing it through stiff resistance. If you keep cranking, the cable will tie itself in knots. Instead, reverse direction gently. When you feel the cable right itself, pull it out and check for damage. If you see no damage, crank the cable into the clog again, working forward and back. Many drain lines require several passes to break up enough of the clog to allow water to flow through.

dishwashers

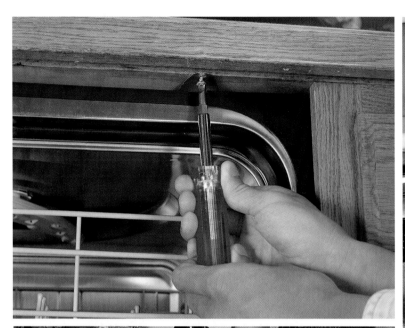

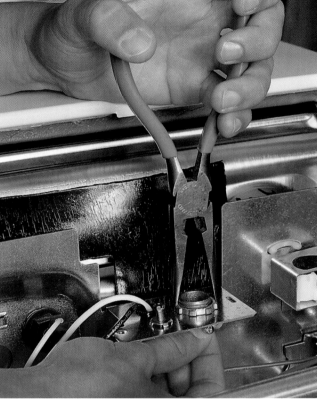

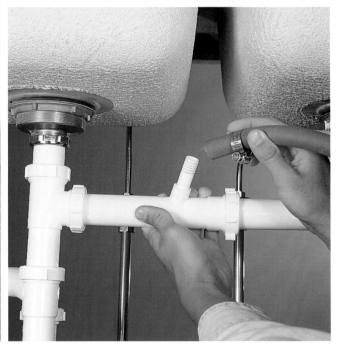

Removing an Old Dishwasher

If you're replacing a worn-out dishwasher, you'll need to remove the old unit before you can install a new machine. Turn off the dishwasher electrical circuit at the main breaker panel, and turn off the water at the shutoff valve.

You'll see a small access panel on the lower front portion of the dishwasher. Look around the perimeter of the panel for hex-head and/or slotted screws that hold it onto the frame of the machine. Remove the screws, and pull off the panel.

Next, you'll have to disconnect the water supply, the drain, and the electricity. Get a bowl or small pan, and place it under the 90-degree elbow of the water supply. Using an adjustable wrench, unscrew the compression nut holding the water supply tube to the elbow, and disconnect the tube. Hold the tube over the bowl or pan, and pull it back and down, free from the front of the dishwasher. Next, disconnect the drain hose just to the right of the water fitting, and allow any excess water to drain into the bowl. Finally, remove the cover of the machine's electrical box, and disconnect the wiring by unscrewing the wire connectors. Pull the circuit cable free of the machine.

With the water, drain, and power disconnected, carefully pull the old machine out and away from the cabinets. You may have to shimmy the machine out of the opening little by little until it's free.

Removing an Old Dishwasher

1 Begin by removing the old dishwasher's front access panel. Look for several hex-head or slotted screws holding it.

2 Have a pan or bowl handy when you disconnect the water and discharge lines. Drain the lines into the bowl.

3 Disconnect the brackets screwed to the underside of the countertop, and carefully pull the dishwasher out by the door.

SMART TIP

When installing a dishwasher, you may find that the unit you purchased comes with the discharge hose already attached. If yours doesn't or if your installation has the dishwasher farther away from the sink than normal, you'll need to purchase additional hose to complete the installation. If you can't find a discharge hose, automotive heater hose is a reasonable substitute you can use in a pinch. Because it is made for car engines, it can easily handle prolonged exposure to high water temperatures and detergent. If your dishwasher's owner's manual does not specify the size hose to use, take a piece of your discharge hose to the store with you to get the right size.

Installing a New Dishwasher

Tip the dishwasher on its back. If it did not come with a discharge hose, attach 6 feet of hose to the purge pump's nipple, and secure it with a hose clamp. Feed the hose through the back of the unit's frame.

Next, you'll need the water connector, a 90-degree elbow with ½-inch MIP threads on one side and a ⅜-inch compression fitting on the other. Wrap three rounds of pipe-thread sealing tape counterclockwise around the threads of the fitting's ½-inch side, and start the elbow into the threaded port of the solenoid valve. Tighten the fitting until it feels snug. Stop when the ⅜-inch side points toward the dishwasher's purge pump.

If local codes allow a direct electrical connection, install a cable connector in the unit's electrical box and pull the wires out of the box. If the codes require a flexible conduit hookup, make this a conduit connector.

Leaving the dishwasher for a moment, drill water, waste, and power access holes through the side wall of the adjacent sink cabinet, just above the floor. Position the holes vertically, tight against the back wall. You'll need a 1½-inch hole for the water and drain lines. If the electrical feed line will pass through the sink base, you'll also need a ¾-inch hole for the conduit. (If you need to run a new circuit to this location, see "Installing a Waste-Disposal Unit," page 70, for instructions.

Push a 5-foot length of ⅜-inch soft copper through the hole, and center the tube in the dishwasher opening, flat against the floor. Lay the electrical cable next to it.

Tap into the existing faucet piping by replacing the existing hot-water shutoff valve (or compression adapter) with a ⅜ × ⅝-inch dual-outlet valve. Shut off the water main, and

Installing a New Dishwasher

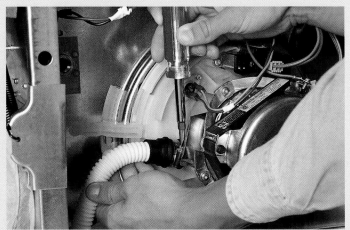

1 Attach the discharge hose to the dishwasher's pump, and lock it firmly in place using the supplied hose clamp or grip ring.

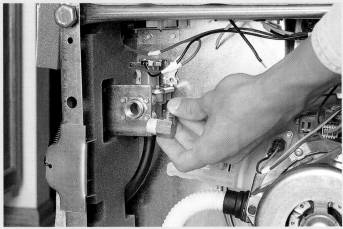

2 Thread a dishwasher elbow into the solenoid valve. Use pipe-thread sealing tape, and wrench it until it's snug.

5 Remove the existing hot-water compression valve (or adapter) from under the sink, and install a new dual-stop valve.

6 Slide the dishwasher into the space. Stop several times to pull more cable and pipe into the cabinet as you proceed.

drain that part of the system. Remove the faucet supply tube; loosen the compression nut securing the existing valve (or adapter); and remove the valve. Lubricate the compression ferrule left on the riser using pipe joint compound, and install the new dual-outlet valve using the existing compression nut and ferrule. Then use the valve's ⅝-inch port to feed the faucet and the other to feed the dishwasher.

If you plan to hook up the dishwasher's drain to a waste-disposal-unit nipple, remove the plug from the nipple and discard it.

If your sink does not have a waste-disposal unit, disconnect the sink's P-trap, and cut a dishwasher drain T-fitting into the waste-kit assembly. This fitting (plastic or chrome) usually goes between the drain assembly's T and the trap, but if it won't fit there, you can splice it into the horizontal tube that joins the two sink drains.

With the water, drain, and electrical hookups prepared, place a cardboard panel in front of the dishwasher and return the unit to its upright position. Orient the back of the dishwasher to the front of the opening; then pull as much of the discharge hose as possible through the largest hole in the cabinet's side wall. Slowly push the dishwasher into the cabinet opening.

Remove the cardboard, and adjust the leveling legs using an adjustable wrench. Raise the dishwasher until its fastening brackets come to rest against the bottom of the cabinet's upper rail or the countertop's edge-band and the unit is level. With all four legs touching the floor, the front sides of the dishwasher should run parallel with the cabinet stiles. When the dishwasher is level, screw the front brackets in place.

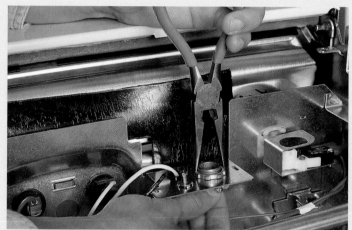

3 Install a cable or conduit box connector in the unit's electrical box. It is required by the National Electrical Code.

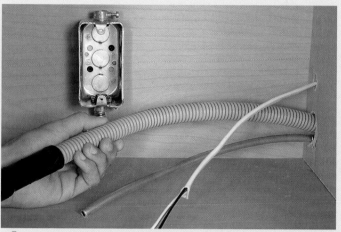

4 Attach a box in the cabinet (if needed), drill a hole in the cabinet side, and pull the water and discharge lines and electrical cable through.

7 With the dishwasher in place under the countertop, thread the leveling legs down with an adjustable wrench and level the unit.

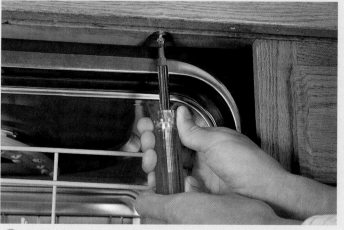

8 With the unit positioned and leveled, screw the fastening brackets to the bottom of the countertop's edge band.

continued on page 108

continued from page 107

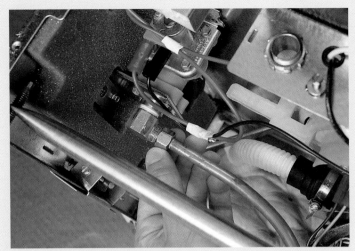

9 Slide a compression nut and ferrule onto the ⅜-in. copper water supply line, and connect the line to the dishwasher elbow.

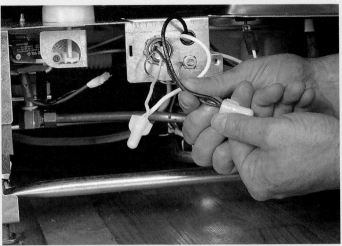

10 Join like-colored wires in twist connectors. Bond the grounding wire under the green ground screw.

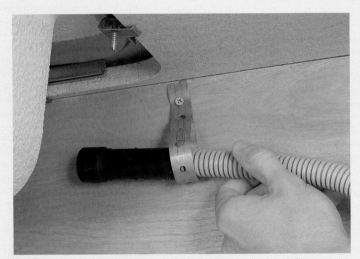

13 The discharge hose must connect to a backflow preventer or loop up to the top of the cabinet, secured with hole strap as shown.

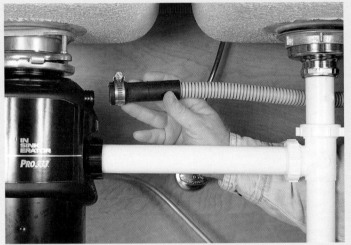

14 Attach the discharge hose to the waste-disposal-unit nipple (if applicable). Be sure to punch the plug from the nipple.

To make the water connection, bend the copper supply tube to meet the dishwasher's elbow. Slide the compression nut and ferrule onto the tube; lubricate the ferrule with pipe joint compound; and thread the nut onto the elbow. Tighten it one turn past finger-tight.

To complete the electrical connection on the unit, attach the conduit to the box connector, strip about 6 inches of sheathing from the cable, and strip about ⅝ inch of insulation from the wires. Tighten the bare grounding wire under the ground screw in the box, and using wire connectors, join the dishwasher lead wires to the circuit or switch-leg wires, black to black and white to white. Then replace the box's cover plate.

Moving back into the sink cabinet, hook up the electrical single-pole switch if you're using one. Connect the conduit and cable to the box, and strip the wires. Join the wires using wire connectors, and pigtail the grounding wires to the box. Attach the black wires to the switch: circuit wire to the brass screw and switch-leg wire to the silver screw. Then fasten the switch to the box using screws, and attach a cover plate.

Trim the copper water supply tube to length, and join it to the remaining port of the dual valve using a compression nut and brass ferrule. Turn on the water so that the connections are under pressure while you finish the job. Any leaks should appear within the next 10 minutes.

Codes require one of two backflow prevention methods for the discharge hose. Either install a backflow preventer, or bring the hose up near the countertop level and secure it there. If a backflow preventer is mandated, you can install it

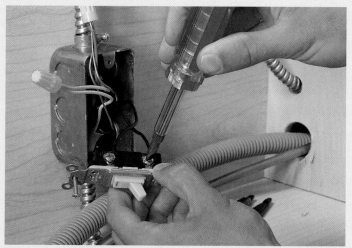

11 Attach the black wires to the switch (if you're using one). Join the white wires in a connector, and bond the ground to the box.

12 Install the dishwasher water supply line in one port of the dual stop valve, and connect the faucet supply tube to the other.

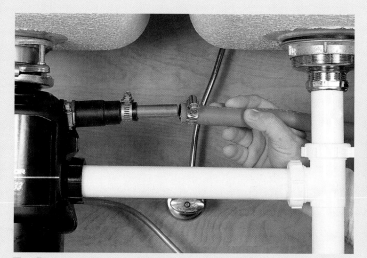

14a With ⅝ in. rubber (non-ribbed) hose, connect to the disposal unit using an adapter.

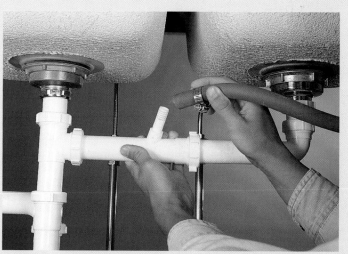

14b If you don't have a disposal unit, use a waste T-fitting.

in the fourth deck hole of the kitchen sink or in a new hole drilled through the countertop, near the sink deck. If an elevated loop will suffice, clamp it just beneath the countertop using a conduit strap: bring the hose up in a loop, pass it through the strap, and screw the strap to the bottom of the countertop or the back of the cabinet. A ⅝-inch wood or drywall screw is long enough to do the job and short enough to avoid piercing the laminate. In any case, don't just run the free end of the hose into the waste-disposal unit or the sink's waste T-fitting. If you do and the drain backs up, the overflow will spill into the dishwasher.

If the discharge hose is a factory-supplied version, it will fit right over the drain nipple on the waste-disposal unit. Secure it with a hose clamp.

If the discharge hose is ⅝-inch heater hose or a factory version very much like it, you'll need a dishwasher waste adapter. These rubber couplings are sized to fit the waste-disposal-unit nipple on one end and are stepped through several sizes on the other. To make the hose-to-adapter connection, trim off several steps with a knife so that the discharge hose fits inside the rubber adapter. Then secure it with a hose clamp.

While this method usually works, the adapter is pliable enough to allow a kink, so a better way is to splice a 3-inch piece of ½-inch copper pipe between the discharge hose and the adapter. The outside diameter of the pipe fits perfectly inside the hose and the smallest adapter size. Hose clamps hold it all together and keep the adapter from kinking.

If you don't have a waste-disposal unit, install a drainpipe with a dishwasher T-fitting and attach the drain hose to it.

glossary

Adapter A fitting that connects two pipes of different sizes or materials.

Aerator The diverter/screen unit that is screwed onto the end of a faucet to control splashing.

Air chamber A vertical, air-filled pipe that prevents water hammer by absorbing pressure when water is shut off at a faucet.

Backflow A reverse flow of water or other liquids into water supply pipes, caused by negative pressure in the pipes.

Backflow preventer A device or means that prevents backflow.

Ballcock A toilet-tank water-supply valve, which is controlled by a float ball.

Branch Any part of a pipe system other than a riser, main, or stack.

Branch bent A vent pipe that runs from a vent stack to a branch drain line.

Caulking A waterproofing compound used to seal plumbing connections.

Cleanout A removable plug in a trap or a drainpipe, which allows easier access for removing blockages inside.

Closet bend A curved drain pipe that is located beneath the base of the toilet.

Closet flange The rim on a closet bend by which that pipe attaches to the floor.

Corpcock (corporation stop) The first shutoff in the water line that is tapped directly into an iron or plastic meter main and can be reached only by excavating the soil above it.

Coupling A fitting used to connect two pipes.

CPVC Chlorinated polyvinyl chloride; a plastic pipe used for hot-water lines.

Diaphragm Used instead of stem washer, this is found on compression faucets.

Diverter valve A device that changes the direction of water flow from one faucet or fixture to another.

Drain Any pipe that carries waste water through a drainage network into the municipal sewer or private septic system.

Drainage network All the piping that carries sewage from a house into the municipal sewer or private septic system.

DWV Drain-waste-vent; the pipe system used to carry away waste.

Elbow A fitting used for making directional changes in pipelines.

Escutcheon A decorative plate that covers the hole in the wall in which the stem or cartridge fits.

Female thread The end of a pipe or fitting with internal threads.

Fitting Any device that joins sections of pipe or connects pipe to a fixture.

Flapper valve A valve that replaces a tank stopper in a toilet.

Float ball The hollow ball on the end of a rod in the toilet tank, which floats upward as the tank fills after flushing and closes the water inlet valve.

Flush valve A device at the bottom of a toilet tank for flushing.

Flux A material applied to the surfaces of copper pipes and fittings to assist in the cleaning and bonding processes.

Gasket A device used to seal joints against leaks.

Hanger A device used to support pipe suspended from a framing member.

Inlet valve A valve in a toilet tank that controls the flow of water into the tank.

Joint Any connection between pipes, fittings, or other parts of plumbing system.

Lavatory A wash basin located in a bathroom or powder room.

Lift-rod A device that opens and closes pop-up stoppers.

Main Principal water or drain pipe to which all household branches connect.

Main vent (or stack) Principal vent to which branch vents may be connected.

Male threads The end of a fitting, pipe, or fixture connection with external threads.

No-hub (hubless) connector A fitting that connects pipes by means of neoprene sleeves and stainless-steel clamps.

Nominal size The designated dimension of a pipe or fitting; it varies slightly from the actual size.

O-ring A ring of rubber used as a gasket.

Overflow tube A tube in a toilet tank into which water flows if the float arm fails to activate shutoff valve when the tank is filled.

Pipe sleeve A clamp used to patch pipe leaks.

Pipe support Any kind of brace used to support pipe.

Plumber's putty A material used to seal openings around fixtures.

Pop-up valve A device used to open and close drains.

Potable water Water that is safe to drink.

PVC Polyvinyl chloride; a plastic used to make cold-water pipe.

Reducer A fitting used to join two pipes of different diameters.

Relief valve A safety device that automatically releases water due to an excessive buildup of pressure and temperature; used on a water heater.

Riser A water-supply pipe that extends vertically.

Shutoff valve A device set into a water line to allow for interruption of the flow of water to a fixture or appliance.

Soil stack A vertical pipe that carries waste to the sewer drain; also, the vertical main pipe that receives both human and nonhuman waste from a group of fixtures including a toilet or from all plumbing fixtures in a given installation.

Soldering/sweating The process used to join copper pipe.

Stack Any vertical main that is part of the DWV system.

Tap A faucet or hydrant that draws water from a supply line.

Temperature and Pressure relief valve (T & P) Device that prevents temperature and pressure from building up inside the tank and exploding.

T (tee) fitting A pipe fitting that is T-shaped and has three points of connection.

Thermocouple A safety device that automatically turns off gas flowing to the pilot if the flame goes out.

Threaded sweat adapter Used to install cold-water pipes.

Trap The water-filled curved pipe that prevents sewer gas from entering the house through the drainage network.

Tripwaste Lever-controlled bathtub drain stopper; two kinds: pop-up or plunger.

Valve seat The part of the valve into which a washer or other piece fits, stopping the flow of water.

Vent stack A vertical vent pipe.

Waste Discharge from plumbing fixtures or plumbing appliances.

Water drain cock A device that allows the water-heater tank to be drained.

Water hammer A knocking in water pipes caused by a sudden change in pressure after a faucet or water valve shuts off.

Wax gasket A wax seal used to seal the base of a toilet so it will not leak.

Y (wye) fitting A fitting used in drainage systems for connecting branch lines to horizontal drainage lines; also provides cleanouts.

index

Glossary/Index

index

photo credits

All photography by Merle Henkenius (CH),
except as noted.

All illustrations by Frank Rohrbach, except
as noted.

page 15: Gary David Gold/CH

page 18: *top left* John Parsekian/CH

page 19: Brian C. Nieves/CH

page 43: *illustrations* courtesy of American
Standard

page 76, 80, 82: *all* Freeze Frame Studio/CH

page 87: *bottom illustrations* by Ian Warpole

page 95: *illustrations by* Clarke Barre